VISIBLY BRILLIANT

HOW TO GO FROM TECHNICALLY BRILLIANT TO VISIBLY BRILLIANT

BY ESTHER STANHOPE

PUBLISHED BY THE IMPACT GURU • LONDON

Published by
The Impact Guru
esther@estherstanhope.com
www.estherstanhope.com

Text © Esther Stanhope 2025
Illustrations © LMPP Studio 2025

The right of Esther Stanhope to be identified as the author of this work has been asserted by her in accordance with the Copyright, Designs and Patents Act 1988

All rights reserved.
No part of this publication may be reproduced, stored in or introduced to a retrieval system, or transmitted in any form or by any means (electronic, mechanical, photocopying, recording or otherwise) without the prior written permission of the publisher.

To find out more about Esther Stanhope, please visit **estherstanhope.com**

Follow her on twitter/X **@EstherStanhope1** and Instagram **@estherstanhope**

Cover and book designed by LMPP Studio
lmppstudio.co.uk
Printed by Ashford Colour Ltd

Paperback ISBN: 978-1-0681958-0-8
eBook ISBN: 978-1-0681958-1-5

Esther Stanhope — Author

"Are you ready to get a massive confidence boost? Read on"

TESTIMONIALS

"Esther is a brilliant force for good who knows how to help others shine. She has excellent insight into all the tips and tricks that make the difference between professional visibility or being overlooked no matter how hard you work."

Viv Groskop, author of How to Own the Room, comedian, and award-winning jouralist.

"Esther is the perfect person to share her wealth of knowledge when it comes to helping professionals to be more visible and pitch themselves. With her broadcasting experience she really knows what she is doing, and she has been a huge help to me."

Dr Suzi Godson, Times columnist, and Co-CEO of the Tellmi mental health service for young people

"Whether you're in the corporate, public, or creative side of the world, Esther's tips will help you smash any speaking gig and feel confident. She's a brilliant speaker, lights up the room."

Dr Vanessa Vallely OBE , Author of Heels of Steel, and Founder of We Are the City

"Esther should come on prescription from the NHS – she's utterly brilliant and inspirational."

Clare Murray – Founder & Managing Partner of the law firm CM Murray LLP

THIS BOOK IS FOR YOU IF YOU

- Are technically good but feel a little bit invisible at work

- Work really hard but don't seem to get promoted

- Feel uncomfortable "bigging yourself up"

- Know you "should" be on LinkedIn but don't "feel it"

- Avoid public speaking or being in the spotlight

- Resent "loud mouths" – the people who seem to get promoted but aren't as technically good as you

- Fight to get a word in, then give up because you don't seem to have the respect or gravitas to be taken seriously

- Want to be seen as a thought leader but don't know where to start

- Want to be recognised for your talent

WELL... YOU'RE IN FOR A TREAT!

INTRODUCTION — ARE YOU READY?
HOW TO USE THIS BOOK

PART ONE

WHY YOU SERIOUSLY NEED THIS BOOK (I DID!)

★★★★★★★★★★★★★★★★★★★★★★★★★

Chapter 1: My story ... I was invisibly brilliant! — 13

Chapter 2: Are you a secret superhero – one of "The Invisibles"? — 17

Chapter 3: Didn't get promoted? — 25

Chapter 4: How I "do" visibility! — 29

Chapter 5: One-a-day inspiration! — 39

Chapter 6: What my TEDx talk taught me about my own "Visibility" — 45

Chapter 7: NOT TRUE! Myth-busters about putting yourself out there! — 49

PART TWO

WHERE ARE YOU NOW, MY FRIEND? AND WHAT'S HOLDING YOU BACK?

★★★★★★★★★★★★★★★★★★★★★★★★★

Chapter 8: The Visibly Brilliant QUIZ! — 55

Chapter 9: Time to set your VISIBLY BRILLIANT Goal! — 63

Chapter 10: What's holding you back? — 71

Chapter 11: Are "THEY" holding you back? — 75

Chapter 12: Does fear hold you back? — 79

Chapter 13: Do YOU hold YOURSELF back from stepping into the spotlight? — 83

Chapter 14: Does gender and diversity play a role in holding you back? — 88

Chapter 15: Does laziness stop you from putting yourself out there? — 90

Chapter 16: Cynicism can stop you from "selling yourself" — 92

Chapter 17: Are you too busy to be Visibly Brilliant? — 96

Chapter 18: Is there a language barrier? — 99

Chapter 19: I.S. imposter syndrome holding you back? — 102

Chapter 20: Perfectionism could be holding you back — 105

PART THREE

WHAT YOU NEED: THE AMAZING VISIBLY BRILLIANT TOOLKIT

★★★★★★★★★★★★★★★★★★★★★★

Chapter 21: The fantasy formula for being Visibly Brilliant — 113

Chapter 22: SHARE yourself (even if you feel naked!) — 115

Chapter 23: HOW to share your stuff! — 127

Chapter 24: Digging for content gold — 143

Chapter 25: Storytelling — 147

Chapter 26: How to make this into content gold — 151

Chapter 27: Dive into the detail of the Triple A Formula! — 153

Chapter 28: What to wear! — 167

Chapter 29: "Chunkology" – gather juicy chunks of content every day! — 175

Chapter 30: Shark Week – how to create yours! — 181

HOW TO KEEP UP YOUR VISIBLY BRILLIANT MOMENTUM

★★★★★★★★★★★★★★★★★★★★★★★★

Chapter 31: Momentum – the Visibly Brilliant Bicycle Wheel — 189

Chapter 32: FLOW – feel your Visibly Brilliant motion! — 197

Chapter 33: Success! What does it look like? — 201

Chapter 34: My final story — 205

Welcome to the world of Visibly Brilliant!

This book will help you transform from technically brilliant to Visibly Brilliant. And the good news? You don't need to have a personality lobotomy or pretend to be something you are not! You can do this your way, at your own pace and you won't need to feel embarrassed or self-conscious about "bigging" yourself up.

If you read this... I promise, you will experience a massive confidence boost.

If you are a talented professional who is technically brilliant at your job, I know how you feel. I used to be brilliant at my job yet made a point of NOT showing off about it.

Are you ready to become Visibly Brilliant? Great! You are in the right place. Need more visibility at work? Maybe you're technically brilliant at your job but go under the radar. Need help with confidence and "getting yourself out there" but don't know where to start? Or maybe you need help with finding the courage and content to post, share and speak without feeling naff and fake. Yup. That's why you're here!

I wish I had read this 25 years ago!

With hindsight, I now know I wasn't Visibly Brilliant at my job. I was an invisible superhero. Like you, I worked long hours, grinding away, exhausted and always going the extra mile in the hope that I'd automatically get promoted for my hard work.

Can you relate to that?

Back in the early 2000s when I was a senior producer at the BBC, I worked long hours, often arriving at work at some crippling time in the morning (4am for the breakfast show!).

In fact, like me back then, you may be what I would call an 'over-deliverer'. Aha, are you OD-ing (over-delivering)? Well watch out! It nearly killed me. Before I left the BBC to set up my own business, I know now that I was in denial about over-stretching myself and grinding away at being technically brilliant. I didn't realise I had to be more visible in order to succeed in my career. I didn't know what "visibility" really meant. I didn't realise it was a career requirement. I'd never even heard of the term "personal brand", and the thought of "self-development" felt alien to me, something "others" did.

I used to actively hide in the shadows (and wear "slimming" black, to avoid drawing too much attention to myself), secretly hoping I would be recognised for my brilliance, loyalty, passion, talent and eagerness. I was the one making sure everyone else shone in the spotlight. From singer Sir Cliff Richard to presenter Vanessa Feltz (I launched her radio show), it was my job to go the extra mile so the "talent" would shine on air. And they did.

I wasn't fully recognised for all my hard work because I was too busy... delivering, putting on a good show, making sure everyone else was happy. Sound familiar?

What you actually need to succeed at work (and your career in general) is to be Visibly Brilliant. That's where the money is, right?

Well, here's where you can start your visibility journey. You've made the right choice to read this book and I've got your back. I'm going to help you go from amazing and technically brilliant at your job to amazing and Visibly Brilliant! I'm going to demonstrate how you can shine and be recognised and rewarded (yes, paid more!) for your hidden talents. And there's some great news.

You don't have to become a show-off, a "blagger" (a fake-salesy-type), or bullshitter to do it. I'm going to show how you can shine, just the way you are, without pretending to be someone you're not.

All it takes is one action a day and a slight shift in mindset to unblock whatever is holding you back. Together we are going to say goodbye to the fear of being judged, the fear of being criticised or a feeling of shame that you might be showing off. Together we are going to prepare you to share your brilliance with the world… just as you are, without feeling icky or overbearing.

EASY AS 1, 2, 3

HOW TO USE THIS BOOK

Simply...

Start by getting a dedicated notebook or journal for your Visibly Brilliant ideas. Keep it to hand as you read through the book.

Work your way through the four parts, even if you skim read, because this will help you build the confidence to get to the next step.

Part One – Why you seriously need this book (I did!)

The Visibly Brilliant USP – unique selling point (don't let the word "sell" put you off!). Allow me to convince you to take the Visibly Brilliant plunge with some personal stories and anecdotes.

You'll need to read Part One and stick with it. Trust me, you'll need to change your mindset (just as I did), or you won't be motivated to do the practical stuff later on.

Part Two – Where are you now, my friend? And what's holding you back?
Fun Quiz!! You are going to find out your visibility "grade", rather like a mini assessment. Hey, you are in the right place. If you have a low score now, it's fine – remember, the only way is up!

And we're going to figure out what is holding you back. You'll be delving into the Top TEN blockers that stop you being free to be your brilliant self and share yourself with the outside world without shame.

Part Three – What you need: the amazing Visibly Brilliant toolkit

I'll be sharing all the tangible things you'll need to get yourself out there.

I have hacks, tips, techniques and terrific tricks on how to create EASY content to share; from storytelling to "bigging" up your role. You don't need to be a genius, a creative or a PhD scholar to do this stuff. You just need to get your "sh*t" together, so you are ready to post, share and talk about yourself without stress or pressure.

Part Four – How to keep up your Visibly Brilliant momentum

Don't worry, I've got many tricks up my sleeve!

You will need a clear and easy-to-adopt strategy, and you will need to become familiar with the Bicycle Wheel of Visibility.

This is where you'll practice the one-a-day habit. One tiny step forward each day will take you on the Visibly Brilliant path to suit YOU and the way YOU roll, in the long run.

At the end of each chapter, you can indulge in tantalising tips, tricks and hacks.

Easy as one, two, three…

You'll get the most out of the book if you work through it in chronological order, discovering how you are going to put these tips and strategies into action YOUR way… that's when the transformation happens.

You've got this!

I've got your back…

You'll love the real-life stories and lessons learnt too.

ENJOY!

PART ONE

WHY YOU SERIOUSLY NEED THIS BOOK (I DID!)

★★★★★★★★★★★★★★★★★★★★★★★★★

Ok. Confession time. This is me ***"selling"*** the idea of being Visibly Brilliant to you! Sit back and let me convince you to read this book from start to finish!

I have created a Visibly Brilliant formula for you so you can start your journey – it's an easy-to-adopt and clear step-by-step approach to creating content ready to share, whatever industry you work in.

My approach is designed to put your mind at rest, so you feel confident that you are sharing the right stuff with the right audiences at the right time. All my tricks are inspired by my many years as a senior producer, where coming up with content (easily) and delivering it with ***"va va voom"*** was a daily thing. And I'm not talking about social media content here. I'm talking about sharing your stories and expertise to make you shine internally in meetings, presentations, online and in person. And yes, I will help you talk about yourself in a professional environment, with ease.

The formula of ***"little and often"*** really does work. I often hear comments from clients about going from hating and dreading sharing their content, to looking forward to it and eventually loving it. They go from technically brilliant to Visibly Brilliant without the stress they once dreaded.

That's been my transformation – from hating the spotlight and feeling like a fraud, to loving it and enjoying helping others at the same time. It's changed my outlook on life and my attitude towards sharing in an open and honest way.

Now I can confidently say – I can help YOU.

The world needs brilliant people like you to speak up and get their voice heard. Brilliant people need to be in the spotlight and on conference podiums because they have brilliant things to share – they might even have ideas or the vision to save the planet, save lives, create life-changing innovations, technological advancements and generally, make the world a better place!

Some of my clients are university professors who, despite working to create breakthrough science innovations, remained invisible (until they met me.)

Others are CEOs of global organisations that used to be SILENT! Many got to where they are through hard work, qualifications, even more qualifications (yes, many needed to feel worthy by studying MBAs and PhDs) as well as diligently working their way up the system. However, before taking the Visibly Brilliant plunge, no one had heard from them or read about them because they were too afraid to be out there, doing PR or speaking in public. Luckily, they realised it was their duty to share themselves and they were able to make the transition from technically brilliant to Visibly Brilliant.

You've probably picked up this book because you know there's something more you could be doing for yourself – not in the sense of working harder, you already work hard and are very good at what you do, you're technically brilliant – but something more, beyond the hard slog. You want to be recognised and rewarded for what you do. And why not? You know it's time to do something about it.

You may have had a wake-up call or been overlooked at a major event or promotion. Or perhaps you've experienced a more gradual awareness that you are being overtaken by others and generally underappreciated and not getting what you want at work.

Maybe you've noticed that others, technically equal to you, are out there getting far more credit, kudos and opportunities than you. You know they also enjoy the pay cheque that comes with that! You're fed up and want your life to change.

By reading and implementing what I'm about to show you, you'll have the secret sauce to create a whole new experience at work.

And guess what? You can achieve this without feeling like a fraud. If you are willing to take the time to learn the steps, I can teach you how to be Visibly Brilliant.

MY STORY... I WAS INVISIBLY BRILLIANT

Picture this. I'm on the red carpet – George Clooney's there, Madonna's here, The Spice Girls are giggling, and Danny DeVito is lighting up the room with his effortless charisma

"Hey, you're looking good," he beams. (He's tiny and very hairy!)

I started my career as a showbiz reporter on the radio in London. In 1996-97 I interviewed every active celebrity at the time; Hollywood stars, rock stars, sporting legends, you name it, I gathered a soundbite from them.

I worked my way up to senior producer at the BBC and made LIVE shows with three British Prime Ministers.

You can just imagine – I was the person holding the "idiot board" (a large script in big writing) encouraging the nervous looking "talent" to perform on camera. I'd count them in...

"Go on, you are wonderful, darling... 4 3, 2... EYES AND TEETH... Action!"

Presenters would fight over me at the BBC. They used to call me the "Star-maker" because I would always get a really good performance out of them, which guaranteed good reviews and a better gig next time. *"You're only as good as your last show,"* they'd say.

Everyone assumed I was this mega-confident person!

BBC News flash...

I wasn't. I wasn't confident when it came to putting myself in the spotlight.

The first massive career-shattering wake-up call came when I was invited to go for a promotion at the BBC for a more senior role.

Suddenly, there I am... quite literally in **THE SPOTLIGHT**. I find myself sitting across the boardroom table opposite eight people, including my boss, my boss's boss, my head of HR and several more people writing notes... all judging me for this career-changing interview!

I feel like a lamb to the slaughter.

No longer am I this confident and competent person. I choke, lose the ability to speak... English (even though that's my only language) and the confidence drains from my body. My mind goes completely blank. It's a horror show.

I know now that I used to suffer from what's called "Glossophobia" – the fear of public speaking (Glosso, the Greek word for tongue... phobia). In fact, if you search "Goodbye Glossophobia" online, you will see my terrified face – the image from my first book!

I feel guilty for not preparing enough that day. However, this is the big light bulb moment... This is the moment I realise I have to change.

The problem was, I was so used to being behind the scenes preparing other people to be Visibly Brilliant, I'd NEVER prepared myself to be comfortable in the spotlight. I didn't even think I had to. I had been avoiding the spotlight my whole life.

I WAS INVISIBLE; technically brilliant at my job, yes, but not Visibly Brilliant!

For more than 20 years I could make others shine on TV, so I knew HOW to make others be Visibly Brilliant but found it impossible to do it myself. I knew how to make other people look, sound and feel confident, but I struggled with it. I was not comfortable in the spotlight, and I had a long way to go.

Another BBC News flash... I didn't get the senior position on that occasion but it was a blessing in disguise...

I left the BBC a short while later to set up my own business, The Impact Guru... why? To help people from all over the world to go from technically brilliant to Visibly Brilliant; leaders, techies, lawyers, bankers, publishers, artists, architects, CEOs, CFOs, hard workers and many hugely talented professionals who miss out on opportunities... because they forget to invest in themselves – and their own career visibility.

Do you know what I call these hidden talents?

"The Invisibles" – the next chapter is dedicated to them!

> ***Terrific TIP*** – Decide now if you want to be more visible. If you do... READ on!

CHAPTER 2

ARE YOU A SECRET SUPERHERO – ONE OF "THE INVISIBLES"?

The Invisibles – they sound like superheroes, don't they?
(Cue superhero music and a Wonder Woman pose!)

You can spot the superheroes a mile off... I used to be one...

- They work harder than everyone else (just like me)
- They wear dark clothes – usually black or navy in the office (like dark superhero capes)
- They hide in the shadows – comfortable behind the scenes, busying themselves with their 35-strong to-do list
- They say things like, "I care about my team, I don't need to be in the spotlight."
- You ask them, "Will you work on Saturday?"
- They respond, "Yes, I work all the time" (because they always go the extra mile)
- "I don't have an ego; I'm here invisibly holding everything together!"

These unsung superheroes are often responsible for invisibly running the entire global organisation!

But The Invisibles aren't usually getting recognised, rewarded or paid enough for all their hard work.

I was an invisible and I'm still on the journey to being comfortable backing myself! To be honest, I've found it painful venturing outside my comfort zone. I still shudder sometimes when I'm about to post my newsletter or share something online.

> **Tender TIP** – My first big tip of the day is simple... get help! Reading this is your first step.

Having another "Invisible", preferably a colleague or ally to back you up and help you to come out of your shell, makes a massive difference. I used to struggle with speaking up in meetings and speaking in public. I used to dread any form of self-promotion... now I enjoy most of it; writing, posting and public speaking. I speak at least twice a week and feel compelled to help you on that journey too.

That's why I decided to write this book... to encourage The Invisibles to come out of the shadows and into the spotlight.

Visibly Brilliant is designed to help brilliant (yet invisible) professionals to:

- Transform from technically brilliant to Visibly Brilliant
- Sell themselves without feeling naff or "icky"
- Speak up in meetings and not get talked over by the "big gobs"
- Shut out the voice of doubt
- Find their voice so people listen
- Share great content and ideas (without feeling like a show-off)
- Get promoted
- Go from fear of failure to free to be fabulous
- Feel effortlessly confident, ready to take on the world

Visibly Brilliant is simply the idea that we all need to be seen. No matter who we are, how old we are, where we are from, and what industry we're in, we all want to be acknowledged. We want to be **VISIBLE** and rewarded for it.

And we're not talking about social media, being an "influencer" with Botox and enhanced buttocks, or seeking worldwide fame – this is about being seen within our area of expertise, raising our profile internally in our organisation, or simply being seen as an expert in our sector.

If we are seen, people can find us, support us, celebrate us, hire us, promote us and share with others.

This book is designed to help you come out from the shadows. It's about "strategic visibility" to help you become successful on your terms. If you don't feel you can be more visible and go around punching the air all the time, that's ok. I often fall off the Visibly Brilliant wagon and don't feel like posting, sharing or taking selfies for months on end. I'm not a natural at this stuff, I'm not always 100% "on" because I'm not always motivated to tell people how brilliant I am (because I don't always feel it!). I am human; but I know how to hack the system by creating processes, habits and small chunks of content to share regularly! I've learnt that consistency is key. I still struggle with my self-promotion. However, I have found a way to keep on track. I'd like to help you find the process of "getting yourself out there" so it's **ENJOYABLE, NOT EXCRUITIATING!**

I'm going to help you find your way to strengthen your profile with consistency and confidence to fit your daily to-do list. There's not ONE WAY to raise your profile, there are many. Being a "big mouth" or show-off is not the only way to shout about yourself and your achievements. There are so many other things you can do that will suit your personality. It all starts with baby steps, so don't give up too early, hang on in there and hear me out.

A quick reminder of why you need to be Visibly Brilliant...

- To be recognised for your hard work
- More opportunities (gigs, promotion, clients, customers, leadership positions)
- Respect
- Getting the credit for YOUR work rather than it going to other people
- More credibility
- To be chosen for the good stuff
- More money!

Let's not beat around the bush. There's no downside to being more visible in your field. You will be more successful if you are. However, please don't be put off by these "salesy" words. You will be in control of your own plan and strategies, so there is no need to panic about trying to be a naff salesy pretend "woo-hoo" type of person.

People who struggle (like the old me at the BBC) with the idea of being Visibly Brilliant have this instant feeling of resistance. That resistance is extremely strong. I remember thinking,

"Shut up, shut up, I know I should be more visible and raise my profile in order to grow and succeed in my career, but I hate having to do this self-promotion CRAP!"

Back when I was a highly respected radio and TV producer, before I started my own business, I just didn't get it. I resisted any form of "leadership-speak" and dismissed personal development as something "other people" (who wore smart clothes and sounded clever) did.

This emotional reaction is common. It can be triggering to hear the following from HR, your boss or your mentor:

"Now you really need to think about promoting yourself and showing off your achievements. Go on, big yourself up or you won't be taken seriously as a leader. Toot your own horn!"

I used to think, "Oh help, not that career-building bilge they always go on about, I think I'll cover my ears La, La, La, I'm not listening!"

The truth is – finding your Visible Brilliance isn't such a biggy. It's not some "fancy pants" magic art that only loud extroverts can do. In fact, the good news is that introverts can be brilliant at being Visibly Brilliant once they know how to play to their strengths (they are often extraordinarily talented at presenting).

It's totally within your reach and it honestly doesn't have to be painful, cringy or naff.

Listen up! Please take your hands away from your ears!

If you don't share a bit of what you do and remain invisible, no one will know what you're doing, and you won't get any credit for it. If you're not seen and heard then you're unlikely to be chosen, picked, hired, offered stuff, invited, promoted or recommended via word of mouth.

So why not make it easy for people to pick you?

It's time to stop being invisible, step out from the shadows and into the spotlight. It's time to take a deep breath, start venturing outside your comfort zone and start sharing yourself with the outside world one step at a time; blogging, vlogging, posting, "podding" (podcasting), speaking, writing, introducing, hosting and generally being seen. Remember, start small, one step at a time, *you don't need to do everything right now.* However, you do need to take the first step... Time to take a breath and dive in!

> **Tactical TIP –** One step at a time, don't try and climb a mountain in one day...
> **"Slow and steady wins the race"**

Aesop's famous fable, The Hare and the Tortoise, tells the story of a race between a slow-moving tortoise and a fast-running hare. The hare, confident in his speed, takes a nap during the race, allowing the tortoise to win. The fable teaches the lesson that "slow and steady wins the race"!

CHAPTER 3

DIDN'T GET PROMOTED?

Many people tell me they dread the whole process of having to prepare for a promotion. They dread having to become Visibly Brilliant from scratch. They realise they've not put any thought or effort into raising their profile, then they try and climb a mountain and fake confidence and visibility when they have never cared about it, respected it or nurtured it before.

A few clients have told me they'd rather leave their secure job than feel fake, judged or under pressure to "play the game". To them, having to be visible is a sinister corporate game. That sounds pretty toxic.

Does that feel like you? Do you sometimes feel a little bit resentful that you have to perform like a monkey in a fake environment to show them what you can do?

I've run many masterclasses and one-to-ones with professionals at global firms who struggle with the whole career-ladder-promotion process.

ALL my clients DREAD having to PROVE themselves in front of a dedicated panel, often made up of HR professionals, their boss and even their boss's boss. One of my clients, Suze, confessed to me that she totally unravelled and lost her confidence before her big panel interview moment.

"I just want to leave the firm; I don't want to go through this horrible process. I don't want to be judged, I'm really good at my job, I feel like giving up and going home rather than facing THEM."

The thing about Suze, is she loved working, head down, and getting stuck into her job.

My Story

I've got to confess, when I was a senior producer at the BBC in London and made to jump through hoops to get promoted, I felt exactly the same. I had to prove myself in front of a very intimidating panel, which was an absolute nightmare. I'd never been judged in this way before in my life. I felt as if I was ON TRIAL.

I was tongue-tied, and I couldn't even answer the simplest of questions. I froze and felt very ashamed of my failure to "dazzle" the panel.

I felt let down by my boss because he had always praised my brilliant work as a creative producer who could hold everything together live on air. He appreciated my loyalty and my long hours of dealing with difficult personalities (celebrities and politicians)!

I remember thinking,

"Why are you doing this to me? Why can't you just allow me to take the next step up the ladder; I've earned it, haven't I?"

I know that in large organisations you have to go through due process, but, in my personal experience, that process can be a personality killer! I hated it, it didn't bring out the best in me. I wish I knew then what I know now! I wish I could have read this book about being Visibly Brilliant back then.

Recently, a client from a global accountancy firm confessed to me...

"I don't want to play the game. Why should I schmooz? Why should I network with people when I'm technically brilliant at my job? Why don't the management recognise what I do?"

I shared this with him, something that changed his life...

"The thing is, Stefan, even if you're technically brilliant at your job, you aren't going to get handed a promotion, just like that. You have to work at a promotion, and you have to learn how to sell yourself and the value you bring. You need to be VB – Visibly Brilliant!"

Does that sound familiar to you?

I have spoken to many people at the top: CEOs, COOs, managing partners, and managing directors. I've asked them for their secrets and what they look for when it comes to considering promotions. What they say is often very simple…

"I don't want people to come whining to me with problems [some call this monkeys on your shoulder], they need to come with solutions!"

> **Trailblazer TIP –** *If you can be a short cut to your boss's problems and you have a solution that you SHARE more publicly, you're much more likely to be recognised and this Visible Brilliance will lead to a promotion.*

Promotion secret

"I appreciate it when you come and share an idea with me – don't shy away from senior people, we don't bite. Yes, we are busy, so be succinct."

CEO Global Bank, Paris

Now it's your turn to take control of your career and be Visibly Brilliant as well as technically brilliant at your job. Good luck!

★★★★★★★★★★★★★★★★★★★★★★★★★

ONE THING A DAY

CHAPTER 4

HOW I "DO" VISIBILITY!

★★★★★★★★★★★★★★★★★★★★★★★★★★

My Story: My Visibly Brilliant Routine – and what I'm going to share with you in this book.

When I first left the BBC and founded The Impact Guru, I had ZERO visibility. I had to start my Visibly Brilliant journey from scratch. I was cynical, sceptical and afraid of self-promotion (yuk!). So, if you feel you are starting from ZERO, don't worry, better late than never.

What I'm going to share with you is how I started the ball rolling and the wheels turning.

Here's what I do NOW each day, week, month and year, after **A LOT OF TRIAL AND ERROR.**

My routine has evolved, and I have had a lot of help along the way. I invested in a business coach, Kim Duke from Canada, who seriously turbo-charged my ability to market myself and write content – even when I didn't think I had it in me. I'm dyslexic, for Pete's sake!

Claire Holmes, my VA (Virtual Assistant), is my rock, my colleague, my confidante, who looks after my diary, social media and planning. She also schedules ALL my posts. She is the one who keeps the wheels on track and makes sure I'm hitting my deadlines. She is brilliant.

So here are my daily, weekly and monthly routines to inspire and help you decide how you want to roll.

A - ACTIVATE `START`

B - BRAINDUMP

C - CHOOSE `THIS WAY`

D - DO IT `BANG`

Daily

Every day I do something towards being Visibly Brilliant. Even if it is simply writing a page of my book or half a blog, I do something… anything.

It's been drilled into me…

"One thing a day, no matter how small, just do one thing"

and I am living proof that it does work.

This is how I do it… (you can do whatever you fancy, just take the bits that work for you)

I start with ABCD:

A – Activate – First I do an activity to get my body and mind moving! I do yoga for seven mins before anything else.

> ***TIP –*** You don't have to do yoga; you can do anything that gives you energy. Sometimes it's the slowest, easiest non-yoga-yoga in the world – I'm not a yogi GURU and I'm not perfect. However, I personally find breathing and stretching extremely useful to get myself in the mood to dive into some content, write or plan my next move. Personally, my brain needs my body to activate first!

B – Brain dump. Next, I jot down anything that comes into my head; ideas, actions, useful contacts, content for my next talk. Sometimes I do this before I go to bed. I find this rids my mind of frustrations if I feel out of my comfort zone. Somehow, writing thoughts down (with loads of spelling mistakes!) in a private notepad is freeing, it's like therapy.

I also jot down ideas of what I might write about in future.

> **TIP –** Don't overthink – just write.

C – Choose. The third step is to look at my scribbles, and they're usually a total mess – rather like my old doctor's prescriptions (I could never decipher the words)! I choose one thing from my notepad and expand on that one chunk of "stuff" – it could be content for a blog, email, article, concept to share, story or case study to add to my presentation.

> **TIP –** Choose the one thing you FEEL you can achieve, the first thing that creates a spark.

D – Do it. The fourth and final step is to DO IT. I commit myself to one, two or three things to do that day. I sometimes call these "Units of stuff". When we're both working from home, I say to my other half, Adam, "I'm getting this unit of stuff done, shhhh, give me five more minutes!"

> ***Tiny TIP –*** One unit, one chunk, one thing at a time is the only way I can get my head around getting stuff done. It works, so why not try it today?!

Remember it has taken me over 10 years to discipline myself to get into the habit of breaking things down into bite-sized chunks; I call this the ***"chunkology"*** strategy. I will explain what that's all about later on.

Don't get FOMO (fear of missing out) if you don't feel like you've not got the space in your day to accomplish a routine like this. You will – just be patient!

Weekly

The one consistent piece of Visibly Brilliant content I share is my **FRIDAY TIPS** – you guessed it, on a Friday. This is my NON-NEGOTIABLE weekly share in the form of a newsletter. It's taken me years to grow from a few hundred subscribers to thousands (and growing). However, don't fret. If you don't have a weekly mail out, you can find ways to share consistent content to suit you.

If you work within an organisation, you could post something monthly. The comms people will bite your arm off for relevant articles with industry knowledge.

Friday Tips is written on a Monday, as well as my Monday Mission I share for my online club.

I have always told myself to keep Monday free from active client work – for writing, planning, working ON the business and visibility, and it pretty much works out. It's become a habit after more than 10 years.

My Friday Tips used to be monthly. Initially all I had to do was write one blog a month and this became the content for my monthly newsletter, plus a couple of posts on social media (LinkedIn).

I remember when Kim, my coach, asked me to write the newsletter every two weeks; I almost died of fear and worry that I'd not have time to write the content. Or I'd not have ideas to write the content.

Then I realised that all the lovely content I was creating could be spread across several newsletters, hence it became weekly. I was still worried people wouldn't like it, or think it might be junk or irrelevant. However, it turns out the tips (on public speaking, confidence, leadership and pitching) are useful, and the tone of the email is fun as it's a Friday!

People often comment, *"I love your Friday Tips; I know it's the weekend when your email comes through... I look forward to your Friday email!"*

Ha! I thought they'd hate it. I was wrong. Can you imagine, I almost didn't have a mail out because I thought I wasn't good enough to write something that people would want to read.

BIG REVEAL – *my weekly Friday Tips is my MASTER chunk, and it gets sliced and diced into other platforms.*

The chunks I create for my Friday Tips are also shared across the board via...

- Keynote speeches – 2-3 times a week
- Social media – 2-3 times a week
- Presentations – cool slides, stats and juicy stuff
- Conference talks
- Media interviews or guest articles

Monthly

Across an average month, I tend to plan and create in batches!

- Batch filming for social media. Hey, if you're not in the mood to make mini videos for Instagram or create internal content – do it in batches. Sometimes I do it every three months

- Speaking at conferences – probably once or twice a month

- E-Publisher – Bookboon, Access Group live virtual classrooms once a month

- Planning cycle – monthly meeting with Claire – I always look at the next four weeks

Now this routine gets easier and the good news is... the more you do, the less you have to do next time.

Tenacious TIP – Schedule Visibly Brilliant time into your diary. You may not know what to do at first but focusing on being Visibly Brilliant for a few minutes a day will help move the dial or unblock procrastination.

If you plan to write one article or post – make sure you schedule one hour as if it's a meeting or a phone call in your diary. I know that it is hard to give yourself time; I struggle with this more than anything. However, respect your own time and invest in your time; make it happen!

Yearly

Plan ONE BIG SPLASH per year.

For example, a book launch – a big event, a new project, a promotion.

I call this **"Shark Week"**. When I worked in TV, we'd call our summer bonanza **"Shark Week"** even if it had nothing to do with sharks!

What we meant by that was the ONE week that you wanted people know about – the big focus, the NEW thing, the amazing "can't-miss launch" and so on.

If you think about it, all you need is ONE big story per year to talk about with your colleagues, bosses, dinner party guests, friends, family and anyone who says,

"How's it going? What are you up to this year?"

It's great to have ONE interesting new thing to talk about.

"We're launching this new product and I'm leading the project."

Or **"We're releasing the next gen model/writing a book/starting a podcast."**

I always have something on the boil each year; book launch/audiobook/special conference keynote/TEDx talk.

What's your Shark Week going to be in the next year?

Hey, don't worry if it feels huge and scary like a big white shark; you can do one small thing a day to get you there and you will. I can feel it in my bones. There's a whole chapter on Shark Week inspiration coming up in Chapter 30.

> **Ta-Da TIP** – Today I dare you to comment on or share an interesting article online – go on, dip your toe in the water! People will appreciate it if you share something you like.

START YOUR JOURNEY

CHAPTER 5

ONE-A-DAY INSPIRATION!

★★★★★★★★★★★★★★★★★★★★★★★★★★

"What do I physically have to DO to be Visibly Brilliant?" you may be thinking.

How do you do it? You simply follow my instructions and do one thing a day.

First though, here's where you START DOING it…

Your one thing today… grab a pen and jot things either in your dedicated notebook or at the back of this book!

Start with a story… it's the best place. Sharing a story is incredibly powerful in meetings, presentations, posts and general water-cooler conversations. Here's some inspiration for you to start RIGHT NOW.

Start by answering these questions… on the theme of "Firsts".

First though, here's where you **START DOING it…**

1. Think of yourself at school. Do you remember the first time you decided what career path to take? What were your dreams?

2. Do you remember the first time you met your boss/colleagues? What were your first impressions?

3. What was the first professional project you led – or felt very proud of?

4. What was the first big career lesson you learnt? (Good or bad)

Pick one of these firsts... Then start your story with "I remember the first time..."

Find an image that might illustrate this – could just be a graphic of a date, a laptop or even better, an old picture of you.

Now use this story in your next meeting, presentation, share with colleagues, write a post or simply save it in a folder ready to use at a later date.

> ***TIP 1*** – It doesn't have to be perfect. This is to dip your toe in the water and get you writing, speaking and sharing stories about yourself.
>
> ***TIP 2*** – If you like all four "firsts" – write them up and save them for later.

Answer these questions on goal setting:

1. Where do you see yourself in terms of visibility in the next one to three years?

2. Choose an event or conference where would you like to speak, or host a panel.

3. Imagine youself in five years, having just got promoted. What kind of image would you like to see of yourself on LinkedIn or the trade press, alongside the heading "Award Winner for Female Leader of the Year"? What does the picture look like? What are you wearing?

4. What's your favourite answer from above? What's the one thing you could do to get one step further to that goal?

TIP: There's no right or wrong answer!

In the US they always have Shark Week *(see Chapter 30, page 181)* where they make every program about sharks on TV because sharks sell!! In the UK we called our "special week" Shark Week even though it had nothing to do with sharks! It's a great concept. This will help you focus on ONE thing to shout about this year!

1. What's the one thing you'd like to shout about this year? A promotion, move, job change, conference speech, book, podcast or award?

If you don't have anything, think about something you could create yourself, like a CEOs' breakfast, wellbeing event, charity walk, or a special event for International Women's Day.

2. What else could you do to maximise your Shark Week? Post on LinkedIn, email senior people, get some press, work with internal comms to promote it to your peers, raise money for charity?

3. Think about last year. What was last year's Shark Week? How can you maximise this (rinse and repeat) to share your insights, knowledge, stories, lessons learnt?

When my first book came out, I had an excellent Shark Week, and maximised every bit of it; Coming up... It's out... The launch... The Amazon impact... The reviews... The next year I had the audiobook and so it goes on. I'm still dining out on my Shark Weeks from years ago!

> ***TIP –*** If you think "extracurricular activities" like leading the graduates' charity run isn't good for business, think again. It's helping you to be more visible if you use it wisely. Doing events, speaking at conferences or hosting B.D (business development) drinks helps you build the skills you need to come out from the shadows as one of "The Invisibles".

ONE-THING-A-DAY INSPO!

Often people ask... where do I start?

Here are some question triggers to get you started... jot down notes on these...

- **What do I really want?**
- **Who am I?**
- **How do I want to show up?**
- **What do I want people to say about me when I'm not there?**
- **Coffee:** speak to senior/ helpful people over coffee.
- **Grow your super network to find "Visibles" who can champion you**
- **Find an ally today –** send them an email.
- **Gather more stories** about your career/projects/people you've helped.
- **Makeover** – put your coloured cape on and come out from the shadows.
- **Journal** – buy a dedicated notebook for your Visibly Brilliant ideas.
- **Bio and headshot** – it's a must so just do it! Book a photographer.
- **Credibility "sprinkling" in comms.** Check out your emails, or any comms, bios you have and see where you can name-drop or maximise your credibility.
- **Credibility** "sprinkling" in meetings.

- **Pick three stand-out achievements –** make them into three slides/posts/stories.

- **Pick three superpowers**/strengths you have and write about them.

- **Personal Brand Max –** interview friends, colleagues, old bosses and family about what is brilliant about you... yes, it's feels embarrassing but this is your project. Find out what people are saying about you and decide how you can use it to your advantage.

- **Childhood stories**, fails, discoveries, hang-ups, life lessons, fun stuff – these will come in handy. Write about them in your journal.

- **TBT – Throwback Thursdays** – post or share something from the past. Dig out those old photos!

- **FAQs –** what are the most frequently asked questions you are asked in your role? Write them ALL down. Choose the best one and create a chunk of content/post/presentation slide with an image.

> ***Thoughtful TIP –*** Think about what you can do to move yourself forward from this chapter, and if you don't get round to it or you feel overwhelmed, take a break. It's ok... do one thing tomorrow. Make it small.

★★★★★★★★★★★★★★★★★★★★★★★★★

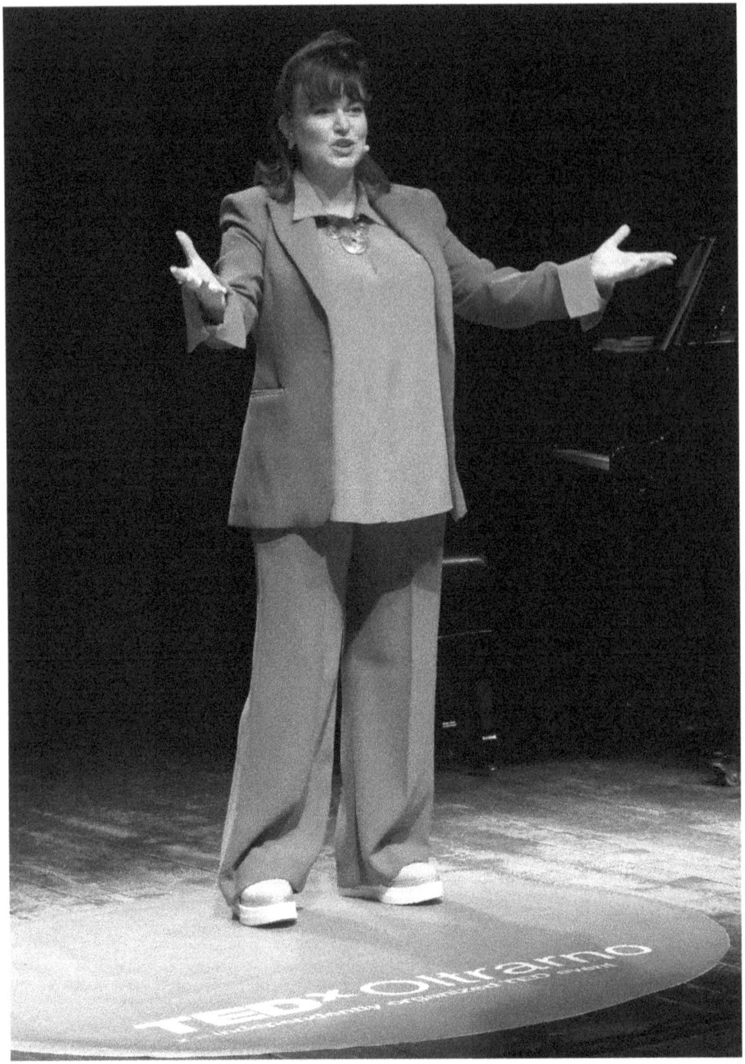
TEDxOltrarno

CHAPTER 6

WHAT MY TEDX TALK TAUGHT ME ABOUT MY OWN "VISIBILITY"

★★★★★★★★★★★★★★★★★★★★★★★★★

My Story

My TEDx talk in Florence was one of the most nerve-wracking, wonderful, painful, soul-searching and exhilarating things I have EVER done in my life. I remember agreeing to do the talk six months before the actual 'curtain up' moment.

I knew in my heart of hearts it would be a real challenge for me, being an extrovert, wing-it-wonder type of personality. The style of TEDx – filmed in one take, with a learnt script, and a stringent time limit – would push me to the very edge of my comfort zone, so I got help.

I created nine chunks of content and a rough flow, then shared my talk strategy on Zoom with my mate Jeremy Nicholas, an accomplished speech coach and comedy writer. He was impressed that I was prepping so far in advance. He liked my content ideas and put my mind at rest. I knew I needed that outside validation in order to build up the courage to do it. I was crippled with self-doubt. I kept talking to my inner-VOD (voice of doubt) and telling it to **** off. I questioned myself daily. However, I fought my inner demons and imposter syndrome by focusing on the "job at hand".

Actor Elia Nichols, a fellow TEDx speaker in Florence, was also a massive support for me. OMG I was soooooo nervous. I remember Elia doing a vocal warm-up in the theatre before we went on stage that night, and I felt like I was having an out-of-body experience.

Hey, I survived! And I'm still here to tell the tale!

The funny thing is, doing the TEDx talk totally stretched my own comfort zone and attitude towards my own visibility. It did terrify me; sharing yourself with the outside world (posting and speaking in public), rather than focusing on your daily job (in the safety of the shadows) takes courage, hard work and self-belief. It's scary.

Personally, I had to dig deep to find my own inner-confidence, self-belief and courage to stand on that stage and expose myself to the live audience – and accept the recording! There's something a little bit terrifying about being recorded as "live" seems very final; you can't change it or edit it. You don't get a second chance. It's a mind ****.

What have I learnt?

You've got to push yourself if you want to grow. Of course I can work hard, that's my default – if in doubt, work; I LOVE working extra hours and feeling busy. I still find myself reverting back to my comfort zone of work, work, work! However, doing something like a TEDx talk forces you to face...

- YOURSELF
- YOUR DEMONS
- YOUR INSECURITIES
- YOUR CORE VALUES
- YOUR INNER CONFIDENCE

It's a real rollercoaster of emotions and I loved and hated stretching myself to the max.

My wish?

To inspire more people to stretch their comfort zone, transform from technically brilliant to Visibly Brilliant and get their voice heard.

The good news is that…

You DON'T need to do a TEDx talk to be Visibly Brilliant!

That was my way of stretching myself because, as a professional "speaker" and expert, I felt I had to prove myself.

There are so many ways you can be visible in your business, as you'll see as you read this book. You WILL be inspired!

> ***Trouble-free TIP*** – You can choose something from Chapter 31 to keep your Visibility wheel turning

★★★★★★★★★★★★★★★★★★★★★★★★★

MYTH BUSTER

CHAPTER 7

NOT TRUE! MYTH-BUSTERS ABOUT PUTTING YOURSELF OUT THERE!

★★★★★★★★★★★★★★★★★★★★★★★★★

You may immediately feel resistant to the notion of stepping outside your comfort zone and pursuing your Visibly Brilliant journey. I used to kick and scream at the thought of posting content and speaking in public. I honestly hated the thought of having to "put myself out there".

I resisted all of this at first. I was so busy doing my job, unaware of the long-term consequences of being brilliant and invisible. I just didn't think any of this stuff was important.

To put your mind at rest, here are a few of the MYTHS that might hold you back from finding Visible Brilliance…

★★★★★★★★★★★★★★★★★★★★★★★★★

1. It will NEVER work, it hasn't in the past, I've tried all this, it doesn't work!

NOT TRUE! This is a long-term gain. Little by little, your profile builds slowly and consistently. Visible Brilliance doesn't happen overnight with one or two attempts at exposure; it only works if you give it time. "Slow and steady," remember! It's a marathon, not a sprint.

2. Tall Poppy Syndrome

In Australia and New Zealand, "cutting down the tall poppy" is sometimes used by business entrepreneurs to describe those who deliberately criticise other people for their success and achievements.

You may be worried that, *"If I become too successful, my peers will criticise me and cut me down to size! I might come across as one of those annoying 'Look at me!' kind of people. People will think I'm showing off and lose respect for me."*

NOT TRUE! Being Visibly Brilliant isn't about being "better" than others. It's about being generous with your knowledge, ideas, insights and stories. What if your peers praise you? What if you share ace content that's useful and interesting and full of golden nuggets that people love?

3. I need to be like Esther who is obviously visibly confident, an extrovert, colourful and a "natural" at this stuff.

NOT TRUE! NO, NO, NO, please do NOT try and be like me. You don't need to be anything like me – being Visibly Brilliant is about YOU finding your own way of being brilliant, raising your profile and giving you the freedom to be yourself.

Please don't think you need to be like me – argh!

4. People will HATE me, I might get trolled.

NOT TRUE! If you share some useful insights and stories that help and teach people, why would they hate you? Trolls are usually obsessed with themselves and their own weaknesses. Would it be a good idea to let trolls block you long-term?

5. My boss and others will think I'm not technically good because I'm wasting my time trying to be in the spotlight.

NOT TRUE! Have you specifically asked your boss? Have you explored the notion that your clients might like your posts/articles or events that you host, and it may attract more business?

6. I'm boring. People won't want to read my content, as I'm not interesting. I'm not a natural storyteller/speaker/writer. Isn't a newsletter perceived as "junk mail"?

NOT TRUE! No one is boring if they don't want to be. You can share interesting content!

7. Isn't this for salesy types ONLY? I'm not a blagger or a bullshitter.

NOT TRUE! Visibly Brilliant is for everyone and anyone who want to thrive and be noticed for the brilliant work they do.

8. It takes too much time to be Visibly Brilliant, I'm too busy doing my real job.

NOT TRUE! Ten minutes of focus time a day is all it takes! Little and often will make a massive impact on your career long term. That's an efficient use of your time if it gets you to where you want to be more quickly.

9. It's too technically difficult. I haven't got the tools or equipment to create good content – I'm no graphics expert; I don't have the IT skills.

NOT TRUE! Get help, just like you did when you were forced to work from home during COVID. (I have a small team of techies who share my content on multiple platforms. Plus, once you've set yourself up, that's it, no more technical knowledge required!)

★★★★★★★★★★★★★★★★★★★★★★★★★

PART TWO

WHERE ARE YOU NOW, MY FRIEND?
AND WHAT'S HOLDING YOU BACK?

★★★★★★★★★★★★★★★★★★★★★★★★

Perhaps you feel you have tried "all this self-promotion malarkey" before, and the thought of having to be in the spotlight continuously drains you. Perhaps you feel you SHOULD be better at being more visible but are not sure where to start.

Fear not, wherever you are right now doesn't matter. Don't beat yourself up. What you will discover by the end of the book is you can build up your visibility from a standing start. You will take part in the Visibility Brilliant quiz in a moment.

We're also going to discover what's holding you back. I used to feel too busy, too stressed, and a little bit terrified to "put myself out there" without some kind of outside validation or permission to "show off". Hey, don't worry, you aren't going to be forced into anything you don't want to do… particularly show off! Stick with this, it's a slow burn, remember. This book is about what you are going to do from now on.

VISIBLY BRILLIANT QUIZ

CHAPTER 8

THE VISIBLY BRILLIANT QUIZ!

★★★★★★★★★★★★★★★★★★★★★★★★★

Time to find out where you are on what I call the **VISIBLY BRILLIANT** scale. Now let's find out if you're:

- Holding yourself back
- Resistant yet ready to dive in
- Holding self-limiting beliefs
- Squandering your talent
- Full of potential
- Ready to set your goal (and have a bit of fun doing it)

In order to access your own Visible Brilliance, you need to work out where you are now so you can start your journey with a fresh pair of eyes and focus on what you need to do.

Are you down in the doldrums feeling brilliant, but INVISIBLE, like my client Alisha? She shared with me her innermost secret. She admitted that she knew she had hidden talents, superpowers, and self-belief locked up inside but she hadn't shared them in 25 years. She told me she had them in her head yet had never had the courage to "sell herself". She was stuck in working-in-the-trenches mode, working really hard for a global charity. Can you relate to Alisha?

Or do you feel you just need a bit of a nudge to get yourself out there more? Let's find out.

First, here's a simple little exercise you can try right now. It's a rating exercise and the question is:

How Visibly Brilliant are you now?

Rate yourself out of 10 on the **VISIBLY BRILLIANT** Scale: Give yourself marks out of 10 for Visible Brilliance, where 10 is very high visibility and you feel you are pretty good at promoting yourself and 0 is the lowest visibility and you probably feel invisible (like Alisha).

Grab a pen and circle the numbers as you go… then see which numbers come up in these questions. This is a very rough guide and a bit of fun to get you thinking!

Quick VISIBLY BRILLIANT Self-Assessment QUIZ... messes vs successes.

Don't be intimidated by these questions – I often make a mess! And don't worry if you score zero for every question. This is where you might be now but it doesn't reflect where you're going to be this time next year!

Question 1: On a scale of 0-10, be honest... how much effort, energy and thought do you usually put into your own visibility and self-promotion on a DAILY BASIS?

0   1   2   3   4   5   6   7   8   9   10

Question 2: How many times have you spoken to a larger group (more than 25 people) in the last YEAR?

0   1   2   3   4   5   6   7   8   9   10

Question 3: How many times have you been promoted (or moved roles) in the last seven YEARS?

0   1   2   3   4   5   6   7   8   9   10

Question 4: How many times have you been recommended or invited to speak at an event, such as a conference, summit or off-site, in the last YEAR?

0   1   2   3   4   5   6   7   8   9   10

Question 5: How many times have you said "YES" to speaking at a conference, summit, town hall or senior meetings in the last YEAR?

0   1   2   3   4   5   6   7   8   9   10

Question 6: How many times have you really stretched your comfort zone and "put yourself out there" in the last MONTH?

0   1   2   3   4   5   6   7   8   9   10

Question 7: How many times have you been praised publicly (either online or via internal company comms email) for your brilliance in the last MONTH?

0   1   2   3   4   5   6   7   8   9   10

Question 8: How many times have you felt super confident and thought to yourself "Yes, I nailed it" in the last WEEK?

0   1   2   3   4   5   6   7   8   9   10

Question 9: How many times have you appeared in the media/TV/radio/podcast or internal newsletter for your organisation in the last YEAR?

0   1   2   3   4   5   6   7   8   9   10

Question 10: How many times have you posted, re-posted or commented on LinkedIn in the last WEEK?

0   1   2   3   4   5   6   7   8   9   10

This is a self-rating exercise, and not about what other people think!

This is how YOU feel about your level of visibility at work and how much you feel you are "seen" for what you do. Hey, don't worry if you are flatlining on ZERO. I know you are brilliant, you're just not visible… yet!

Wherever you are on the scale now doesn't reflect your future score, or your potential to be 10 out of 10. That's what you're here for. Potential is a wonderful thing; we've all got bags of it. Plus, I know you have bags of talent ready to show the outside world.

Ok, let's see what your VISIBLY BRILLIANT rating might say about where you are now…

Your results! Add up all your numbers and divide them by 10, then write your average result here…

> **Thinking TIP** – *If you swing from 0-10 from question to question and feel a little inconsistent, that's fine, I used to be like that. See how to set longer-term and consistent goals in Chapter 9.*

If you mainly circled 0, 1, 2 and 3 – Hey, don't worry, you are not Visibly Brilliant… **YET!** You will be if you put your mind to it. You are starting from scratch and probably haven't considered "putting yourself out there" yet, because you've been BUSY, BUSY, BUSY, doing your job and honing your important technical skills. That's fine, please carry on getting yourself qualified, skilled up and brilliant at what you do.

What you're going to discover in this book is that you're not required to climb a mountain or to be pushed into knee-jerk reactions to fast track your **VISIBLE BRILLIANCE**. It's a slow burn; remember, slow and steady wins the race. Your visibility will last longer than the Speedy Gonzalez who try to cheat their way into the spotlight like a moth flying into a burning heat lamp! It's time to take that first step – after a while, you'll be rewarded for all your hard work. Remember, all I am suggesting is one thing a day. That's it!

If you mainly circled 4, 5, 6 and 7 – You've got HUGE potential to take the plunge into being **VISIBLY BRILLIANT** sooner rather than later. You are already on the journey to finding your visibility; well done!

You know you are capable of self-promotion, yet something is holding you back. You are probably busy working "in" the business, as opposed to "on" the business or your career. Perhaps you've put your visibility on the back burner because you're getting on with your day job. That's fine. You may not want to be like those "shouty-show-offs" on LinkedIn who "toot their own horn" – in other words, the self-publicists.

It could be that you don't have the confidence to launch yourself into the spotlight yet. You are ready to take the plunge and be seen as a brilliant operator, poised to take on a more senior position or up your game in business! However, you want to do it YOUR way as your authentic self, without compromising your integrity. Don't worry, you will find your Visible Brilliance – we'll be discovering what lies beneath the surface and bring out your brilliance to share with the outside world.

If you mainly circled 8, 9 and 10 – Wow, you are on the right track. Well done!

This is a very useful exercise if you still have something niggling in your head about being Visibly Brilliant. It's reassuring to know you are doing all these things – perhaps you know you are doing well but just need a couple of tips and tricks to keep you motivated?

You can still use the ABCD routine (see page 30) to get your head in the game, no matter how advanced you are. Visible Brilliance is an ongoing journey – with room to grow, build and continue the momentum.

If you are already Visibly Brilliant, thank you for joining me for the ride! You may discover something new in my tips and tricks! (I'm still learning myself.)

Whatever your **VISIBLY BRILLIANT** score is now, don't be too hard on yourself. You will find your Visible Brilliance and when you do, you will know exactly how to position yourself to the outside world. You'll start getting more comfortable posting, sharing and speaking to wider groups. You'll feel more confident entering a room, effortlessly taking up your space, even when the bigwigs are challenging you! You'll soon realise that what feels outside your comfort zone now won't in the very near future. In fact, even if you're a low scorer on the VISIBLY BRILLIANT scale (and I'll bet money on this!), you will start to enjoy the process of finding your Visible Brilliance once you start the journey.

Trust me, I've seen people transform from IN-Visibly Brilliant to Visibly Brilliant when they never thought it was possible!

> **Trust Me TIP** – *No matter where you are on the Visibly Brilliant scale, stick with me. You will reach your goal if you do one thing a day. Promise!*

★★★★★★★★★★★★★★★★★★★★★★★★★★

VISIBLY BRILLIANT GOAL

CHAPTER 9

TIME TO SET YOUR VISIBLY BRILLIANT GOAL!

★★★★★★★★★★★★★★★★★★★★★★★★★★

While this rating is fresh in your mind, let's set some goals. Turn to a fresh page in your notebook or the blank pages at the back of this book and start jotting down some thoughts.

What does good Visible Brilliance look like to you?

Imagine yourself in a year's time – what boxes would you like to tick?

- Had a "glow-up"
- Started your own business
- Launched your new website with photos and videos!
- Gained thousands of folowers
- Won an award (like "most promising leader in IT!")
- Respected in your field as the "go-to" expert

BRAIN DUMP!

So, take your pen out and jot down where you want Visibly Brilliant to take you… don't overthink. You don't have to be perfect.

Here are a few triggers to inspire imagination:

- Need a promotion?
- Fed up being stuck in head-down work mode?
- Want to be seen as a leader or "thought leader" (people look at you and think, "ooh, they know what they are talking about")?
- Considering a book?
- Thinking of running a course?
- Need followers and proof of your expertise?
- Attract more customers in an authentic way (not shouting "look at me" naff marketing campaign)?
- More clients?

Being Visibly Brilliant will get you **SEEN** by the people who need to buy into you, as long as you **ARE** putting yourself out there.

Take the pressure off...

Please don't beat yourself up. If consistency is preventing you from being fully Visibly Brilliant, we can sort that out. Let's start making Visibly Brilliant a habit and getting into that daily routine. In fact, for now, do LESS.

You don't need to leap ahead and get yourself out there posting and filming yourself, only to feel like you want to hide next week. If you feel like you want to hide at the very thought of being on camera – that's ok, YOU ARE NORMAL!! I sometimes feel like that even now. Don't rush into it because if you don't enjoy it, you won't do it. So ask for help or a buddy to team up with to make it more enjoyable.

TAKE IT SLOW! THERE'S NO RUSH.

There's no one size fits all Visibly Brilliant strategy or routine; if you create your own "process" and maybe get a little help, you will feel so much more comfortable and confident about the whole thing.

You aren't necessarily seeking FAME – however, you know that being more visible will be better for you and your business. You're not just doing this for the sake of it because someone told you to *"get on social media"*...

GET CRACKING

Try this practical exercise today

A - ACTIVATE — Your mini exercise, walk or stretch to get your mind, body and soul ready to work.

B - BRAINDUMP — Your vision for YOU in the future; people know who you are, clients come to you, you are asked to appear as a guest on a podcast and/or you are nominated for an award.

C - CHOOSE — Which idea you'd like to focus on starting now.

D - DO IT — Go ahead and write your notes on the next page or create a mood board.

OPTION 1 — WRITE NOTES

Notes

1. By this time next year, I'd like to be………
2. In six months, I'd like to have………
3. In three months, I'd like to have………
4. In the next month, I'm going to………
5. This week, I'm going to start………

- Conference speaker
- Promotion
- Weekly mailout
- New photos and headshots
- Seen as a credible leader
- Chairing the Town Hall meeting
- Glow-up (in other words, you LOOK the part)
- How do you want to FEEL?
- What do people see when you walk into the room?
- How do you look on Zoom?
- Running a networking group
- Investing in a helper!

NOTES

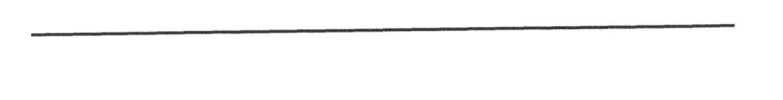

OPTION 2 – CREATE YOUR VISIBLY BRILLIANT MOOD BOARD

You could search for pictures and images that capture your idea of what Visibly Brilliant means to you and put them in a folder, up on your wall or PPT presentation – whatever floats your boat.

You can change your vision any time. This time next year, it might have evolved into something much bigger or more sustainable. You may decide like me, to get help. As you know, my amazing VEA (Virtual Executive Assistant) Claire helps to distributes all my content across different platforms.

Getting someone to help you may be the BIG step you can take to build in that daily/weekly/monthly consistency.

> **Tempting TIP** – *Be flexible. Try new stuff. Be bold because why not? You've got nothing to lose.*

★★★★★★★★★★★★★★★★★★★★★★★★★★

WHAT'S HOLDING YOU BACK?

FEAR

CHAPTER 10

WHAT'S HOLDING YOU BACK?

★★★★★★★★★★★★★★★★★★★★★★★★★★

Confession. I am NOT the perfect Visibly Brilliant finished specimen. I know I have held myself back (and still do sometimes).

My Story

I am inconsistent and struggle to be ok with social media. I am NOT "a natural" – even though many people assume I am "born confident". I am on a journey, and I am still figuring it out. I have worked out a few hacks and tricks to maintain momentum (and keep my Visibly Brilliant wheel turning – this will be explained later on!).

"It's alright for you!" people often say to me. They think I'm ok with being front of camera and on a stage. I am comfortable now; however, it's taken me more than 10 years to get over my lack of confidence and fear of public speaking. No matter what the outside world sees, you have to find your own path. Even the Visibly Brilliant people don't feel like they've cracked it. When people say, *"It's alright for you, because you are confident…"* – it's not entirely true. I'm not 100% confident most of the time. I still have to venture outside my comfort zone a lot.

So why don't most of us feel Visibly Brilliant?

I've gathered responses from hundreds of clients I've spoken to from all over the world. Here are the most common reasons people tell me why they might be holding themselves back. Do any of these sound familiar to you?

10 REASONS YOU MIGHT BE INVISIBLE (YET BRILLIANT)

1. THEM. You don't want to be one of "them," a show-off, arrogant, ego!

2. FEAR. Fear of humiliation, failure, not being good enough and of being judged.

3. YOU. The script running around in your head is holding you back.

4. GENDER/DIVERSITY. In my experience, women and the underrepresented are far more likely to hold themselves back from the spotlight.

5. LAZINESS. Can't be bothered to change the status quo.

6. CYNICISM. Doubt. Not believing in self-promotion. It's for "blaggers" only.

7. BUSY, BUSY, BUSY! So busy doing your job that you have no time for you.

8. LANGUAGE. You may not speak English as a first language, yet you need to speak it in business, so you stay quiet in fear of sounding silly.

9. I.S. imposter syndrome holding you back? That terrible feeling of self-doubt... you feel as if someone is going to tap you on the shoulder at any moment and tell you you're not good enough.

10. Perfectionism! You get stuck because you don't think your material is good enough, so you end up NEVER sharing anything! (I still catch myself being a perfectionist and blocking myself)

> **Tipsy TIP** – *No blame no shame! Stop beating yourself up, you're doing ok.*

This isn't about blame, so please don't feel guilty about blocking yourself from finding your Visible Brilliance. Have you ever heard the phrase, "The truth will set you free"? Admitting this to yourself will help you to move past your block. Before we delve into the "blockers" in more detail, let's face facts: most of the time, we get in our own way! Most of my clients tell me they tend to overthink how they come across which means they chicken out of sharing their stories and expertise in a public forum.

The hardest part of building your Visible Brilliance is this two-parter:

1. Deciding to do it. This means dealing with what holds you back.

AND

2. Investing in yourself. That is, investing in your time, your energy, your efforts and your commitment.

So, let's start with the why! Why aren't you allowing yourself to be Visibly Brilliant?

Let's dive into the truth behind why you still feel invisible.

> **Truthful TIP –** *Be honest with yourself. Why are you holding yourself back? Dig deep and read on.*

★★★★★★★★★★★★★★★★★★★★★★★★

I'M NOT ONE OF THEM

CHAPTER II

ARE "THEY" HOLDING YOU BACK?

★★★★★★★★★★★★★★★★★★★★★★★★★

Them? "The Visibles"? You can't stand the idea of turning into one of "the big gobs".

The "Visibles" – you know they lack technical brilliance, yet they talk a good game. Certain people (who love self-publicity) have probably put you off the idea of being Visible. If so, you are not alone.

I ran a masterclass for a super-talented team in a large techie/engineering firm. I asked the group what the main reason was for not wanting to be Visibly Brilliant. 100% of the 40-strong team admitted that it was "Them" (the show-offs on LinkedIn) that put them off. They all agreed that showing off was vulgar and bad taste.

Do you relate to my talented techies?

What about academia? Surely sensible professors and lecturers aren't big-headed arrogant show-offs?!

Um, oh yes they are. I received this email from a very well-respected professor at an extremely prestigious university... she will remain anonymous.

Dear Esther, I am not Visibly Brilliant, because I don't like most people in the university where I work who often are self-serving and condescending. Their achievements were in the past, and their brilliance is built on being visible, not being brilliant. Cue conflict, since being more visible would be helpful!"

In her view, in the world of academia, there are certain groups of "Visibles" who aren't brilliant at all. Perhaps they were once. They published, researched or discovered something in the past and as a result have been put on a pedestal. They now take it for granted that they are safe in their high-profile positions. They talk a lot, they have a voice, yet they no longer have anything new to say or to contribute. They must stay at the top and continue to be on "important" panels spouting their (old) beliefs to maintain their visibility.

They have the name of the university behind them to prop them up. They have a sense of their own importance because they are associated with the faculty.

In short, these visible but not brilliant people have massive EGOS! What a turn off!

There are so many reasons for this. One of my clients, a founder of a specialist global law firm, tells me that when she started her legal career in a larger traditional firm, she was taught to value herself in terms of the number of billable hours; young lawyers are taught to work long hours and bill clients for every six minutes of time they clock up. They are terrified of not reaching their targets and many fail.

As lawyers, they are expected to be clever, know their stuff and come across as credible and serious. However, when they reach partner level they are suddenly required to win new business and be, what can feel like out of nowhere, Visibly Brilliant.

The trouble with this seismic shift in skillset (and mindset) is that many get left behind. You either sink or swim.

My client admitted that lawyers can be snobbish about people who put themselves in the spotlight, and see those posting on LinkedIn and appearing on panels as "vulgar"– even though this is exactly what's needed to achieve partner level. They often mistakenly think that if you are Visibly Brilliant, you can't possibly be a good lawyer.

The point is, you don't have to be like "them"; the show-offs, the self-promoters and "Visibles" who are not brilliant. Don't allow these arrogant so-and-sos to put you off.

GET CRACKING

Try this quick exercise!

Jot down the answers to these questions in your notebook.

1. Who, in your mind, is Visibly Brilliant without the arrogance?

i.e. they don't show off, they add value or contribute something that helps people. Maybe they share their expertise or tell stories about their life lessons. They could be famous like Oprah or Simon Sinek! However, try and choose someone closer to home – say, a colleague of yours.

2. What do they do to be visible?

i.e. speak on a panel or write a blog. What content do they share?

3. What could you start doing to move in that direction?

i.e. ask them who hosts the podcast, research their producer, or find out who organises the conference guests and put your name forward! (Yes, it is as easy as that, I've done this many times... you may get a "no", however if you ask enough times, someone will say "YES")

> **Talented TIP** – *Do not compare yourself with one of THEM; you are talented in your own way.*

★★★★★★★★★★★★★★★★★★★★★★★★★★

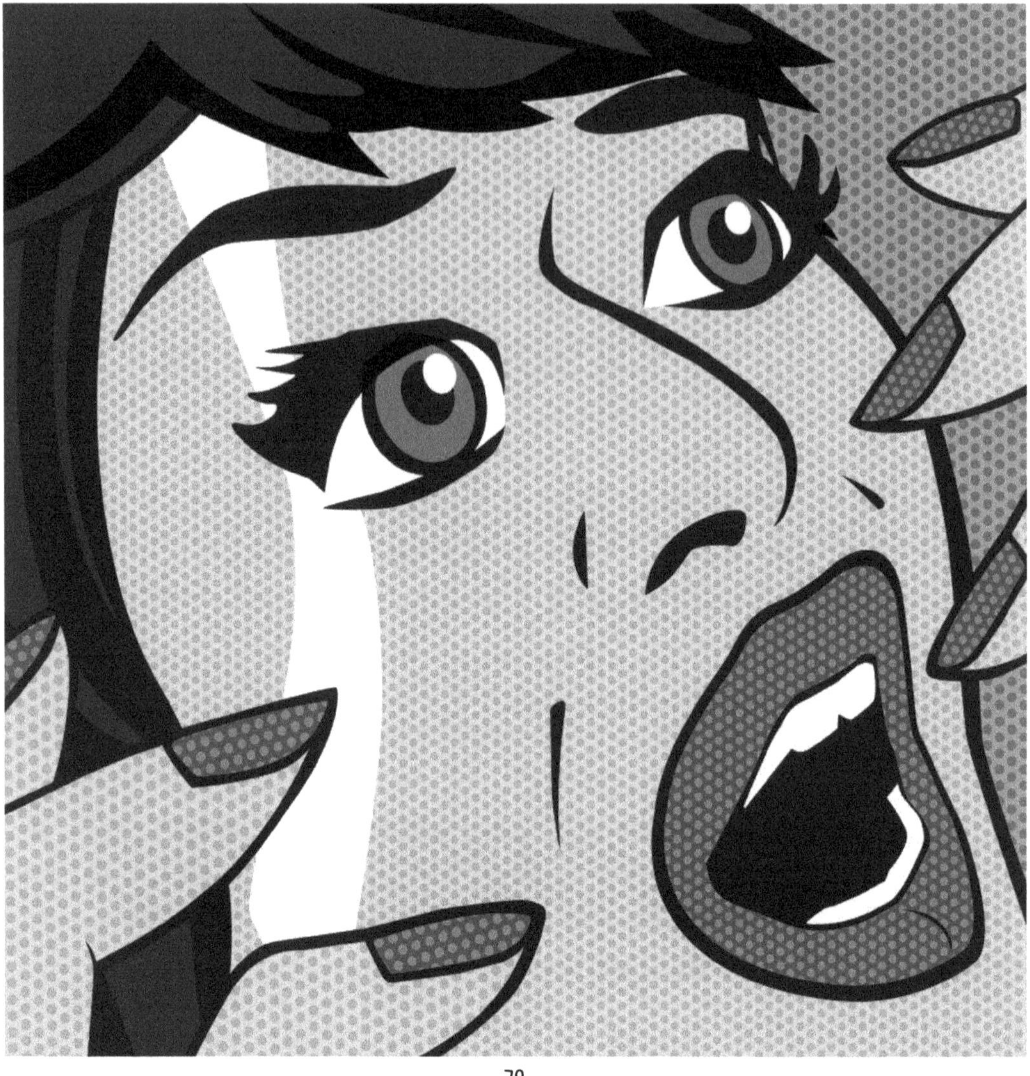

CHAPTER 12

DOES FEAR HOLD YOU BACK?

★★★★★★★★★★★★★★★★★★★★★★★★★

Are you secretly afraid of baring all and getting the wrong reaction? Or feeling like a big disappointment when people respond to you being visible? Are you worried that you will be judged or criticised? Guess what? The truth is… most people feel the same! Fear holds us back. Fear of failure used to hold me back and still does, sometimes.

My good friend and therapist, Olivia James – Performance & Confidence Coach based in London's Harley Street – sees many clients who are afraid of the "backlash" if they put themselves out there.

Olivia shared her client's story with me:

"My brilliant client was reluctant to make videos showcasing her expertise.

I discovered she'd been in a controlling and abusive relationship where she'd been criticised for everything she did. This fear was holding her back years later.

No wonder she was terrified of making videos.

Sometimes we internalise the critical voice of a parent or boss which makes us want to protect ourselves from attack. This can make us hide. Awareness and therapy can help you move past this despite your trauma, and you can be Visibly Brilliant."

Being terrified of making a mistake is very common yet holds so many of us back.

"You're Not Good Enough!" Does that inner voice come and bite you sometimes?

My client Klara is terrified of making a mistake and humiliating herself in front of her professional peers in case they judge her harshly. She is so brilliant at what she does, and she is visible in terms of her senior position on the board and leading global teams. Yet she struggles with the spotlight.

"I'm absolutely terrified at the prospect of being publicly humiliated when it comes to being Visibly Brilliant and standing 'naked' in front of an audience. I'm hugely uncomfortable at the thought of being judged and worried that people will criticise me for my mistakes."

Where do these fears come from? Many of these fears stem from feelings associated with imposter syndrome, the nagging sense that you will be "found out" for not being good enough. These feelings dwarf the perceived benefits of being more Visibly Brilliant so many feel it's not worth the risk.

The thing is, we all make mistakes at times, whether we're visible or not. And the fear of failing is so much more debilitating than failing itself. Because the cliché is true – we learn from our mistakes, or we try another way, or we just get back up a little stronger than before.

If you feel fear at the thought of finding your Visible Brilliance, you are so not alone. And can you imagine how you will make someone else who deserves to be Visibly Brilliant feel if they see you putting yourself into the spotlight a little more?

This book is here to help you create new habits (and new neural pathways) so you can move forward with your visibility, regardless of the negative inner thoughts about yourself (that aren't true, by the way!). The daily Visibly Brilliant routine and strategies are designed to help you dissolve these blocks through practical action. We start small and then increase your exposure! Don't get me wrong – I'm not dismissing these feelings of fear, I'm merely minimising the damage they can cause so you can move forward confidently.

> **Thrill-seeking TIP –** *It's ok to be outside your comfort zone, it's ok to feel fear... when you do you know you're living... you're stretching yourself!*

★★★★★★★★★★★★★★★★★★★★★★★★★

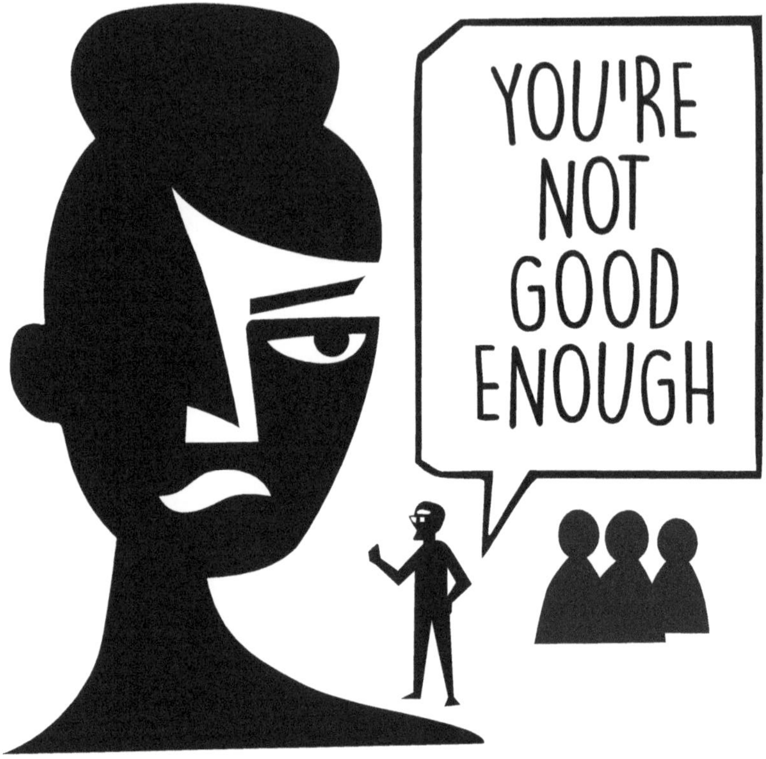
YOU'RE NOT GOOD ENOUGH

CHAPTER 13

DO YOU HOLD YOURSELF BACK FROM STEPPING INTO THE SPOTLIGHT?

★★★★★★★★★★★★★★★★★★★★★★★★

What is the script that starts to run in your head when you think about being more Visible?

- I'm not good enough... I need more knowledge
- I'm not as good as (fill in the blank), they are super confident
- I'm not experienced enough; I don't sound credible
- People think I'm too young, why would they listen to me?
- I'm not an extrovert, it doesn't come naturally
- I'm not articulate enough
- My English isn't fluent enough; I might come across as stupid
- They might judge me or find me out for the fraud I am
- I don't want to send junk mail to people – and p**s people off
- If I risk speaking at a conference, my whole reputation is on the line
- If I work harder and become more qualified, I'll be more confident
- I hate selling myself, it's naff
- I wasn't properly educated at a top university

Hey, it's ok, you're not alone. I used to say ALL these things to myself and still do sometimes. And most of my very senior clients (all over the world) in business, politics, Hollywood and the media tell me they have similar scripts in their head on a loop.

TIP – *Check your inner script. What little "untruths" do you tell yourself?*

WERE YOU CRITICISED AS A CHILD?

My Story

This was my script...

EYES AND TOOTH! ESTHER AGE 6 IN 1978
I wasn't always confident

I wasn't 100% confident at school. I couldn't read aloud, and I somehow felt "less than".

Were you ever criticised as a child? Do you remember a comment that's stuck with you all these years later? It's not simply about the "now" but also what happens in childhood and how these incidents hang over our entire lives.

It's only recently dawned on me that my confidence was damaged very early on when I was around six years old. I didn't want to be visible or "found out" after many negative comments from my great aunt Winifred, a retired schoolmistress.

"Aunty" was a tiny woman with a scary attitude towards children – you always had to be well-behaved as "children should be seen and not heard". Poor old Aunty, she probably didn't realise it was her many comments and "constructive criticism" that made me feel "less than".

Once she even commented on my weight. I remember sitting round the dinner table at her cottage in Norfolk.

"Look at those thick arms."

I'm still traumatised by that comment all these years later.

Then there's the bad spelling issue. She'd talk about her own pupils in her school before the war and how they'd be able to spell. And I remember her telling me she'd write the words "SAID" and "SIAD" on the old blackboard with chalk, and her pupils would know which word had the correct spelling.

Aged six, I remember thinking, "I'm not sure which spelling is correct, I must be so stupid!" I had no idea back then I was dyslexic – it hadn't been invented then! And I felt so silly and unconfident about spelling, speaking and saying the wrong thing in the wrong way, that I held myself back for a lot of my life and career. I struggled with reading and writing, even though I was very creative. In the 1970s creativity wasn't seen as an asset in school.

Touching TIP – *Be kind to yourself, be your own champion, back yourself.*

So that was my script. "I'm stupid"

My editor, Olivia, had a similar experience at school when she was six. In class, she had sewn a small mat in different stiches and colours for her mum. Juliet, the child next to her, had sewn a small soft toy. The teacher made both girls come to the front of the class. Pointing to the soft toy, she said, "Look how beautiful Juliet's soft toy is – so much care has been taken over it!" Then she picked up Olivia's mat by one of the corners, as if it were a dirty rag, and said, "And look at Olivia's, compared to Juliet's!" Olivia will never forget that moment of embarrassment and shame. (Her mum still has the mat all these years later!)

I'm still re-writing my script.

So how did I go from that little, unconfident kid who felt ashamed about being a bit stupid and slow with "thick arms", to a radio and TV producer at the BBC, who now runs a business as a keynote speaker, author and personal impact expert, helping leaders and CEOs all over the world to be more Visible?

The first step is awareness – just allowing ourselves to take a step back and witness the scripts that we all have playing in our heads. The second step is to trust the evidence against the script; a 2.1 Batchelor of Arts (BA Hons) degree at uni, A-grades in exams, multiple awards, accolades, senior roles, celebrity interviews, 12,500 hours of live radio and a successful business! Why would I think I'm a bit stupid?

That's what this book is all about... weaning yourself off your old inner script by putting practical steps in place... including an easy-to-adopt daily routine. When you intentionally focus on positive actions, you begin to rewrite that pesky script.

I've learnt to stop holding myself back and I'm still doing one action a day to keep me moving forward. Stick with me for more ideas, suggestions and inspiration to help you.

CHAPTER 14

DOES GENDER AND DIVERSITY PLAY A ROLE IN HOLDING YOU BACK?

★★★★★★★★★★★★★★★★★★★★★★★★★★

In my experience, having spoken at thousands of gender and diversity leadership events all over the world, people often hold themselves back because they feel they "don't conform to the norm". Often, women tell me they struggle to feel "good enough" to put themselves out there and compete with your typical confident, courageous and articulate types.

This non-conformist community will often admit to not having the confidence to *"put themselves out there"* as easily as their alpha-type colleagues, partly because they don't have the role models to show them the way.

"You can't be what you can't see". (That's the famous Michelle Obama quote!)

The entrepreneur and inspiring co-founder of Little Moons, the mochi ice-cream company, Vivien Wong, uses Michelle Obama's quote and inspiration to spur her on. I admire Vivien as she sees her visibility as her duty to show others that you can be diverse, different and non-typical AND be in the spotlight.

Like Vivien, I'm on a personal mission to encourage women and the less visible superheroes in business to get out there and be seen and heard! So, what's my message to women and the underrepresented?

Give it a go, start now, start small, be brave and read on!

Juliet Blanch, a leading name in the world of arbitration from Arbitration Chambers, sent me this...

"Visibly Brilliant really resonates with me – too many brilliant younger women lawyers (wrongly) assume they will be promoted because their work speaks for itself, not realising or understanding how important Visible Brilliance is."

The award-winning author Gill Whitty-Collins writes about the Umbrella Theory in her book "Why Men Win at Work". She says:

> *The Umbrella Theory and men's generally better grasp of it is coming even more strongly into play as everyone works from home it seems - I guess it was inevitable, given we are all even less visible under our 'umbrellas' to our bosses than we are when we are in the office. Now more than ever, women need to remember that, no, it is not enough just to do great work and assume the people above you will notice: your work needs to be visible and you need to be visible. You need to get out from under the umbrella and make sure your boss knows what you are doing and knows YOU. I know many women thought there would be less networking going on by men because they're not in the office but, I can promise you, not a chance of that. Because men know it's important and they are finding a way - they may not be 'popping by' their manager's desk, but they are for sure 'popping up' on zoom instead. How else do you think they got 3 times more promotions and double the pay rises? We know it's not because they're better, more intelligent, more capable.*
>
> *It's an umbrella thing."*

Thank you, Gill Whitty-Collins, for allowing me to use your quote.

★★★★★★★★★★★★★★★★★★★★★★★★★★★

CHAPTER 15

DOES LAZINESS STOP YOU FROM PUTTING YOURSELF OUT THERE?

★★★★★★★★★★★★★★★★★★★★★★★★★★

Can't be bothered? Or maybe the people who book the show-offs to speak are too lazy to find a new voice!

An old BBC colleague of mine, who now runs his own business, used to put his lack of visibility down to "laziness". He confessed that until he decided to grow his media consulting business, he "didn't feel the NEED" to put himself out there. He was happy and comfortable doing a great freelance job for his trusted clients. He thought he'd been a bit lazy because he was happy operating in his comfort zone and sticking with what he knew.

But there's also laziness when it comes to being "chosen." As a former producer himself (like me), he knows that "those Visible people" are chosen to speak on panels or radio shows because the bookers, journalists and event organisers are simply lazy. They want to book the tried and tested speakers purely because they can't be bothered to try out NEW voices in case they don't perform. It's a vicious circle. How do you get yourself on the conference circuit or in the media without doing a first gig? If the bookers only want people who are already visible, it can be very tricky to take that first leap because you're not yet well known as a good panel guest or contributor.

I know first-hand from booking daily guests at the BBC that the blockage of new talent being seen is down to laziness. We used to use the ENPS (Electronic News Production System).

> **Big Tip Here** – *If you want to be an expert on the radio or TV, get yourself on a smaller, local show first. There are local radio stations all over the world. In the UK, it would be something like BBC Berkshire (in the English countryside), as they are always looking for free guests. Make sure your title is logged as an expert, such as "Leadership Expert", "Climate Change Expert", or "CSO" (Chief Sustainability Officer). Next time someone at the BBC or another media outlet needs a 'talking head' in your field, your name will pop up.*

Sounds simple? Because it is! It's not that the people are amazing or earth-shattering in their performance, but often they are booked because they happen to have their name on the ENPS system, on the email chain, were Googled, or their name popped up and they simply answered the phone!

Laziness from others – the bookers, event organisers, the comms team and the producers – can work in your favour... once you're on the radar. However, you do need to get on their radar in the first place. It's worked for me many times.

> **Thrifty TIP** – *Put yourself out there, no matter how small the step. Get yourself a guest appearance – it could be at a client event, or on a panel.*

★★★★★★★★★★★★★★★★★★★★★★★★★

CHAPTER 16

CYNICISM CAN STOP YOU FROM "SELLING YOURSELF"

★★★★★★★★★★★★★★★★★★★★★★★★★

Don't worry, you're normal!

Hey, bring on the cynics. I get it. I used to be a cynic when it came to having to "sell myself". I didn't buy into the whole Visibly Brilliant phenomenon at first. I didn't think it was relevant to me, and I didn't think I needed to show off or be Visibly Brilliant outside my usual operating area in business. Even when I left my safe staff job at the BBC, I got all my first and trusted clients through word of mouth, so truly believed this was the only decent and trustworthy way to run my speaking and coaching business.

However, word of mouth is only ONE of many ways to get yourself out there. It's a fraction of what you need to be Visibly Brilliant. What I didn't realise then was how important the Golden Pear rule is. It's all about sowing seeds and seeking out opportunities to shine. You need to look beyond your network. If you don't sow seeds for the future, you won't have any golden pears (speaking gigs, promotions or other opportunities) to pick!

In order to be consistently Visibly Brilliant all year round, I had to do more than rely on word of mouth. I had to sow seeds for my pear trees. I had to create and grow golden opportunities myself; in other words...

GROW GOLDEN PEARS!

You can't have empty muddy fields with NO SEEDS or shoots growing and expect to wake up the next morning with a full orchard with shiny, ripe pears (gigs) to harvest! You need to sow, plant, water, prune, wait, nurture, pick and store your lovely golden pears. And the good news? If you nurture, pick and store your beautiful harvest of Visibly Brilliant pears, you can use them all year round. Crunch!

The golden pears you plant, water, nurture, pick and store – they don't appear overnight!

Word of mouth alone does not grow your golden pears.

Someone else who used to rely on WOM (Word of Mouth) is award-winning author of "Write a Bestseller", Jacq Burns, the brilliant founder of the London Writers Club and my personal writing coach and literary agent. She is a high-profile operator in her field of publishing and is hugely successful and "up there" in my eyes. However, could she be more Visibly Brilliant? Yes! She told me, she operates on a word-of-mouth basis. Her initial thoughts behind being Visibly Brilliant were:

"I don't NEED to be famous – I don't NEED to be a show off, I get clients already, I only need to impress a certain group of people and I've done that, so I'm fine the way I am."

However, as she helped me with this book, she realised that she was, in truth, making excuses not to be even more Visibly Brilliant. She found herself reflecting on the time she spent on marketing herself and her business. And she realised that she was very busy, grinding away doing her work in a Technically Brilliant manner (because she is bloody brilliant at what she does). She found she was thriving in her comfort zone (just like me), editing books for clients, running programs, organising luxury writing retreats and filling up her time doing what she loves. It dawned on her that she had been neglecting her potential Visible Brilliance. Through our discussions and by working on the book content with me, she decided to give my Visibly Brilliant tips a go. She started taking selfies and posting them with short comments (something she had never done before) and using my one-thing-a-day trick. She also started thinking about her audience more and all the fantastic tips and insights she could share about the world of publishing (including my Triple A formula for sharing – coming up in Chapter 26). Guess what? It worked!

Another talented professional, a client of mine, Kremera, admitted that,

"I don't need LinkedIn until I start looking for a job."

Ha ha, that's where she was wrong! So many people mistakenly think that you only need to be Visibly Brilliant when you need something back, i.e. a new job, a promotion, or searching for new business or new talent to join your team. But it doesn't work like that. You can't be Visibly Brilliant by clicking your fingers and expect everyone to look at you, click on you and KNOW you, just like that. You have to nurture your profile like the golden pear tree.

> **Timely TIP –** *Start NOW! You can't be Visibly Brilliant overnight; it's a long-term activity. You need to sow seeds, grow them, then reap the rewards… only then can you pick your juicy pears.*

★★★★★★★★★★★★★★★★★★★★★★★★★

CHAPTER 17

ARE YOU TOO BUSY TO BE VISIBLY BRILLIANT?

★★★★★★★★★★★★★★★★★★★★★★★★★

You may be thinking, *"But I have no time to think about being Visibly Brilliant, I'm far too busy running my business, OD-ing (over-delivering) for clients or colleagues and generally serving the interests of others!"*

My great friend, bestselling author, coach and keynote speaker, Zena Everett, writes about "busy-ness" in her books, "The Crazy Busy Cure" and "Mind Flip: Take the fear out of your career".

Zena tells me…

"We are so busy with our heads in the weeds doing our job, that we don't have time to make sure that we are getting noticed. Some of us are even brought up to think that self-effacing invisibility is a desired behaviour. In my book, "The Crazy Busy Cure" I describe how when I was a young girl in Ireland, a long time ago, I was a keen member of our local Brownie pack. We were taught that a 'good' brownie would be a silent helper, never drawing attention to ourselves. We were encouraged to get busy with chores for the family like setting the table, laying the fire (I told you it was a long time ago), tidying up, and that we would get a warm inner glow from knowing we'd been good.

What a load of BS that was. Translate that hard-wired invisibility to the workplace and think of the damage that does to your career. You are not going to get on in corporate life if you are crazy busy doing a good job invisibly.

You are just opening the space for your smartly prioritising and visibly good colleagues to snatch promotion from under your nose."

Thank you, Zena Everett, for your wise words. You are a massive inspiration to me.

GET CRACKING

Try this quick practical exercise!

Answer these three questions – either jot your answers in a notebook or at the back of the book on the Notes pages.

1 – Am I prioritising my tasks? (i.e. how do I make sure I complete the ones that advance my long-term career goals and Visible Brilliance?)

2 – What can I delegate or automate? (i.e. how can I easily offload less critical tasks like proofreading, VAT or anything repetitive such as filing or checking documents, that could free up my time for personal development?)

3 – Are you ready to be Visibly Brilliant? If yes, read the rest of this book and make sure you choose a Visibly Brilliant activity immediately!

> **Tactical TIP** – *Even when you're ridiculously busy, 10 mins a day will help you move forward. Remember, one thing a day, little and often.*

★★★★★★★★★★★★★★★★★★★★★★★★★

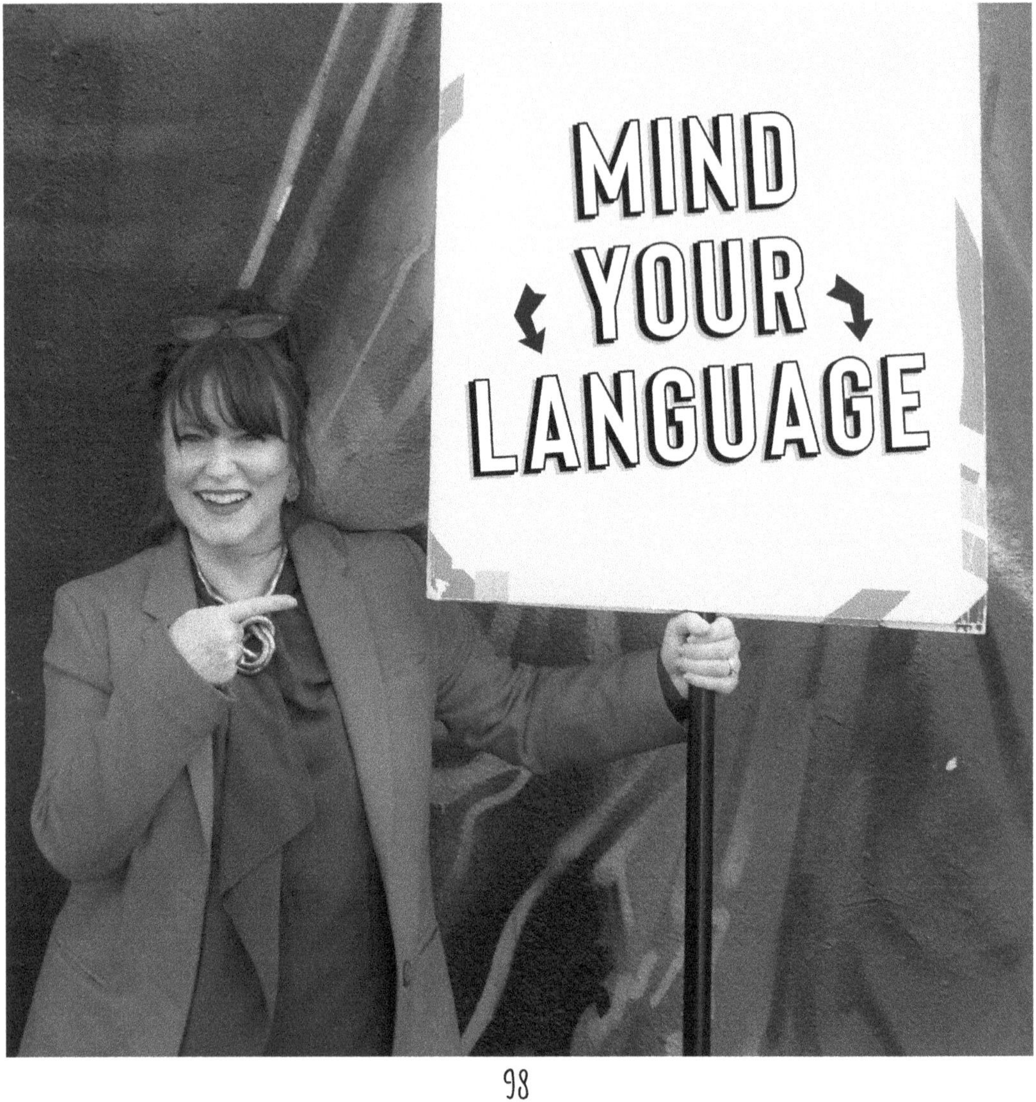
MIND
YOUR
LANGUAGE

CHAPTER 18

IS THERE A LANGUAGE BARRIER?

★★★★★★★★★★★★★★★★★★★★★★★★★

When English isn't your mother tongue, you might lose confidence when it comes to presenting yourself.

Does this sound familiar? You may not speak English as a first language, yet you need to speak it in order to do your daily job because that's what your business requires… so you stay quiet in fear of sounding silly.

Hey, it would be a shame for you not to be more visible because of language when there are so many workarounds to help you.

I was running a leadership summit over Teams recently with clients from the Chinese and Asia offices of a global tech firm (yes, it was very early in London when I dialled in at 6.30am!). When I talked about being more visible in the workplace in order to get noticed, heard, respected and promoted, many of the extremely experienced, senior people on the call told me they couldn't put themselves out there because of the language barrier.

They expressed their frustration by writing in the chat box about why they don't speak up in meetings. Many admitted they don't speak up because their English is too basic and not fluent. Many find the written word easier to translate, so they end up emailing and messaging rather than speaking in meetings. It became apparent they were not used to speaking off the cuff and struggled with finding the right words as they talked to me.

This is a common problem in global organisations. Written communications are fine because they can be translated fast. However, it's very hard to express yourself with confidence when the words don't roll off the tongue.

I often tell my clients who don't feel confident with their English that they need very few words to make an impact. You can still post, write, film video clips and use subtitles to create content. There are many ways to express your ideas. Use AI, and get allies and people to help you.

I once spoke to senior leaders at the BDA (British Deaf Association) and after a few minute of getting help with translating sign language, I realised very few WORDS were required to deliver a strong message. We found a way of communicating with semi acting-speaking-signing and lots of facial expressions.

Words are only one tiny piece of the Visibly Brilliant jigsaw.

A QUICK STORY ABOUT LANGUAGE.

My Story

A few years back, I had the pleasure of attending a beautiful wedding in Spain. The bride was Spanish and the groom was a native English speaker. The bride's father, who was responsible for giving the BIG speech over drinks and cigars, couldn't speak a word of English. The bride stood by him and was asked to translate.

The father of the bride was a prolific bullfighting commentator and wasn't used to having to pause during his commentary but he stood up and delivered this charismatic, heartfelt speech that had the audience eating out of his hand.

His voice was deep and LOUD, like an opera singer. He was 11 out of 10 on the charisma scale and his pauses were breathtaking. He'd stop for a second and change the cadence of his tone. Then pause again and start to weep.

The bride could barely translate because her father kept going without room for the translation!

I was in awe of this fantastic "matador-like" performance. I didn't understand 95% of his words and but it was probably the best speech I have ever witnessed.

I do remember the bride taking the microphone at the end and simple saying, after 10 minutes of hearing his smooth and baritone voice…

"He wants me to say he loves you all!"

There wasn't a dry eye in the house!

The point there is, you can understand a lot just by someone's presence and impact.

> **Lost in Translation TIP –** *If you are able to use a translator or find quick and easy AI shortcuts to help you with the language – DO IT. Do not let language hold you back.*

★★★★★★★★★★★★★★★★★★★★★★★★

CHAPTER 19

I.S. IMPOSTER SYNDROME HOLDING YOU BACK?

★★★★★★★★★★★★★★★★★★★★★★★★★

It held me back for years... that feeling of self-doubt... you feel as if someone is going to tap you on the shoulder at any moment and tell you're not good enough.

Emma is a senior woman in banking, and an amazing leader. She is CONFIDENT on the outside but couldn't put herself out there. She told me she doubts herself, says sorry all the time... (argh, that's a whole book in itself: the use of the word "Sorry" and why women use it ALL the time!).

Quick fix tip.

STOP SAYING **SORRY** — SWAP IT WITH **THANK YOU**

EVERYONE is insecure, it's normal, it's ok to feel a bit "less than" sometimes, you are humble, you are human.

At the BBC I worked with many celebrities, Hollywood stars, prime minsters, and actors. Often, the rich, famous and most charismatic characters suffered from imposter syndrome more than "civilians." They are often paranoid that they are not as brilliant as the character you see on the screen. It turns out that without make up, beautifully designed suits and a fantastically witty script, they are... NOTHING! Well, they feel like NOTHING, compared to the gorgeous superhero up there in lights.

I'd often dread having to produce talk radio shows with actors because they'd sometimes have literally nothing to say... they felt "less than" when faced with their "normal" personality. They would suffer from imposter syndrome in the live studio more than "normal people" because they'd somehow feel they were letting their fans down.

Note. If you feel imposter syndrome is crippling you and your chances of being Visibly Brilliant and think you would benefit from professional help because you're sabotaging your career, there's no shame in asking for it. In fact, if you need therapy (and I am totally pro this), it takes courage to admit it. That's ok. Do whatever it takes to help you move forward.

> **Thoughtful TIP –** *If your VOD (voice of doubt) is holding you back and saying stuff like "You're not good enough" then give it a silly name to take away its power. One of my clients calls hers "Patronising Patty" while mine is "Cynical Cyril"!*

★★★★★★★★★★★★★★★★★★★★★★★★★

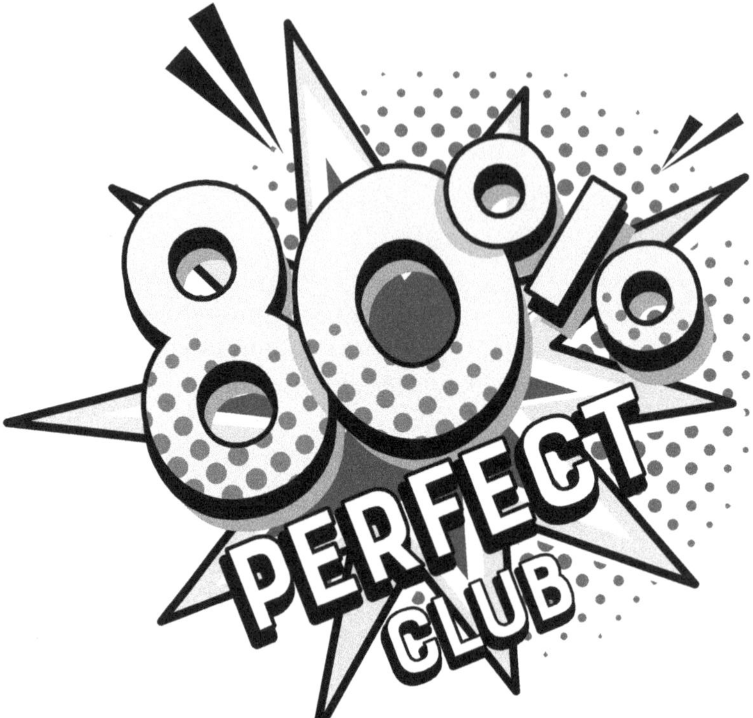
80%
PERFECT
CLUB

CHAPTER 20

PERFECTIONISM COULD BE HOLDING YOU BACK

★★★★★★★★★★★★★★★★★★★★★★★★★

You get stuck because you don't think your material or what you have to say is good enough, so you end up never sharing and become even more stuck!

I confess, I still catch myself being a perfectionist and blocking myself. Sometimes I can't bring myself to press "Send" because I'm not happy with my newsletter or think it's not good enough. I make myself say...

"I'm not perfect, it only needs to be 80% Perfect, just press send" and I do.

I once heard the term "reformed perfectionist", and I love to think of myself as this as it acknowledges the secret inner perfectionist in me, lurking beneath the surface.

Plenty of people I've spoken to about this argue that perfectionism is a good thing because having high standards is a "must" to show credibility and polish. However, if your perfectionism stops you doing stuff, it's dangerous. This kind of "all or nothing" mindset can do more harm than good. It's important to embrace a mindset that values progress, trying stuff out and learning new things, over perfection!

Is your inner-perfectionist guilty of...

- **FOMU – fear of messing up!** Perfectionists often have a deep fear of making mistakes or failing, which can paralyse them from acting.
- **Procrastination.** Perfectionists might delay starting tasks because they feel they don't have the perfect conditions, ideas, or tools to achieve their "perfect" outcome. That's why doing one thing a day is key. If you delay your action because it's not perfect, you'll never get yourself out there.
- **Stress.** The constant pressure to achieve perfection can lead to burnout, anxiety and can affect wellbeing.
- **Curbing Creativity.** The need for perfection stifles creativity and the desire to venture outside your comfort zone. When you're creating content, trial and error and being open to learn new things is key to being Visibly Brilliant.
- **Lowering Self-Esteem.** If perfectionists fail to meet their own high standards, it can result in feelings of inadequacy and low self-esteem.

Get Cracking... Quick exercise to combat your perfectionism... go on!

Have a go at this "BAD" task.

Spend NO LONGER than 10 minutes in total on this exercise. Set the timer on your phone for both tasks.

The idea is to do it without overthinking with one objective in mind – to do this and DON'T TRY to be perfect... In fact, actively do it badly!

Perfectionism Task Part 1 – 3 minutes

Write down in your notebook or back of the book (or scribble messily!) a brief list of all the achievements you can think of both in business and in your school/personal life, no matter how small and in no particular order (i.e. Ballet medal, Grade 8 Saxophone, Wrote an eBook, Promoted to Head of Comms, Talent spotter, Made £5 million for the company last year, Won an Academy Award – you get my drift!)

Perfectionism Task Part 2 – 7 minutes

Pick one achievement from above and answer the following questions VERY quickly without thinking:

1 – When and where was this achievement?

2 – How do you feel about it now, at this moment?

3 – What does it say about the kind of person you are?

4 – What did you learn from it?

5 – What one tip would you give to a younger colleague who is inspired by your achievement?

There… that's a great piece of content gold you can share, post, speak about or simply add to your folder of Visibly Brilliant chunks to use in future.

> **Tasty TIP** – *Take a screenshot of your notes, and put it in a folder marked "Visibly Brilliant".*

And the great news? You don't have to be perfect!

How was that for you?

SO GOODBYE TO

- Being invisible
- Perfectionism
- Work, work, work
- Imposter syndrome
- Voice of doubt
- OD-ing (over delivering)

AND HELLO TO THE NEW YOU WHO IS...

- Confident
- Visible
- Charismatic
- Unafraid to show up and shine
- Free to speak your mind

AND WHO

- Wears what you want in the colour you want
- Says what you want
- Tries new things
- In other words, YOU, with a growth mindset and ready to take on the world!

You'll soon discover that people around you, in your team, your audience and your clients will love you just the way you are, warts and all!

DO YOU WANT SOME MORE GOOD NEWS?

You are over halfway there! You've just got to want to be seen and heard as the brilliant leader you are. You've got to give yourself permission to be Visibly Brilliant. Are you ready?

Good. Well done – you've done the hard part! You're changing your mindset because you are still here! Thank you for reading this far.

Time to share yourself with the world.

> **Tough Love TIP** – *Do something badly! Don't be perfect. Today I dare you to: write a poem, start a post or record your personal elevator pitch in voice notes on your phone. Do it BADLY! It's a great exercise if you suffer from perfectionism (like me sometimes).*

★★★★★★★★★★★★★★★★★★★★★★★★★

PART THREE

WHAT YOU NEED: THE AMAZING VISIBLY BRILLIANT TOOLKIT

★★★★★★★★★★★★★★★★★★★★★★★★

In all my years of broadcasting, producing top talent at the BBC and working with senior executives in business, I have found having a practical and easy-to-adopt formula is REALLY helpful. I've managed to boil done ALL my years of experience when it comes to speaking up, showing up and being… a little bit awesome, into three main themes – my Triple A formula;

A - Audience

A - Authentic

A - Awesome

Standby for everything you need to know!

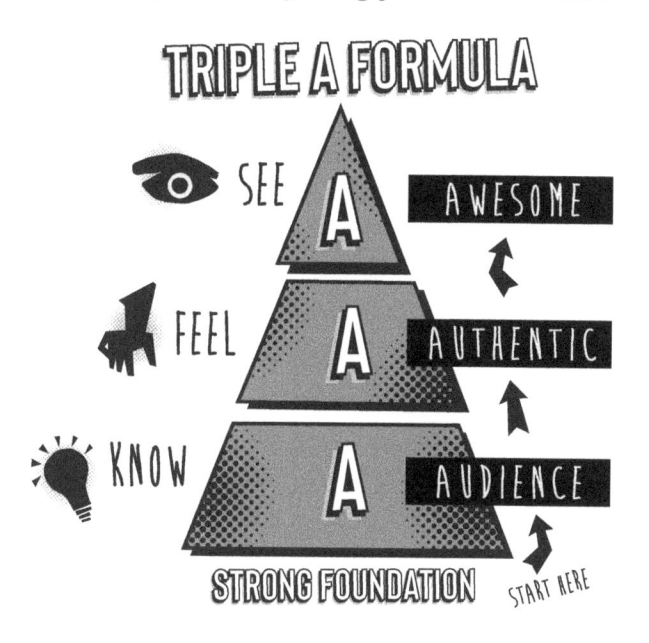

TRIPLE A FORMULA

- 👁 SEE — **A** AWESOME
- ✊ FEEL — **A** AUTHENTIC
- 💡 KNOW — **A** AUDIENCE

STRONG FOUNDATION — START HERE

It makes sharing content that bit easier because the foundation is there for you to follow, step by step.

All the other structures and strategies from S.O.W. to T.E.E.N. will help you create lovely content chunks. You don't need to know EVERYTHING about EVERYTHING to be Visibly Brilliant, but you do need a few tools, ideas and a bit of inspiration to get your head in the game.

This section will help you find YOUR own formula that works for YOUR personal toolkit.

BRILLIANT AT YOUR JOB QUALITY HEADSHOTS
SENSE OF PERSONAL BRAND
GREAT REPUTATION 1000S OF LIKES
SPARKLING WINE (!) PASSION GOOD AT SELF-PROMOTION
BOOK COMING OUT 80% PERFECT OWN IT
SPARKLING PERSONALITY EYE FOR DETAIL
SOCIAL MEDIA
SPEAKS AT EVENTS UNIQUENESS LOTS OF OFFERS
PRESENCE TRIAL & ERROR COURAGE ON THE TABLE TO SPEAK IN PUBLIC
BIRDS EYE VIEW
RESPECT IN YOUR FIELD WELL-WRITTEN BLURB
BRILLIANT ON VIDEO REGULAR ARTICLES IN GLOSSY MAG
STRONG LEADERSHIP QUALITIES
BOUNDLESS ENERGY LOVE OF YOUR TOPIC
GREAT INNER MEDIA APPEARANCES GSOH
CONTENT CONFIDENCE
CHUNKS EYE FOR BIG PICTURE PIONEER SENSE OF FUN
ROLE MODEL TECHNICALLY BRILLIANT = VISIBLY BRILLIANT
INTERESTING BIO NEWSPAPER COVERAGE SHARER

CHAPTER 21

THE FANTASY FORMULA FOR BEING VISIBLY BRILLIANT

★★★★★★★★★★★★★★★★★★★★★★★★★

If you could wave a magic wand and create an instant Visibly Brilliant formula that works today... would it look something like this?

Courage, Brilliant at your job, Sense of personal brand, Great reputation, Respect in your field, Good at self-promotion, Speaks at events, Book coming out, Media appearances, Great content chunks, Uniqueness, Well-written blurb, Social media presence, Passion, Love of your topic, Brilliant on video, Pioneer, Trial & error, 80% perfect, Quality headshots, Interesting bio, Sparkling personality, Newspaper coverage, Strong leadership qualities...

LOL – easy peasy, lemon squeezy. Simple, right? The truth?
There is no fast formula.

Tremendous TIP – *You only need to do one teeny tiny thing towards your Visible Brilliance a day and you will build up your own recipe, no pressure, no sweat.*

SHARING IS NOT SHOWING OFF

CHAPTER 22

SHARE YOURSELF (EVEN IF YOU FEEL NAKED!)

★★★★★★★★★★★★★★★★★★★★★★★★★★

Sharing is NOT the same as showing off. However, sometimes the thought of sharing yourself with the outside world feels scary, and you feel exposed. You may feel like you're opening yourself up to criticism from peers or even slightly toxic friends. I used to think people would judge me if I shared my "stuff".

Please don't confuse sharing with showing off! It's like the difference between confidence and arrogance.

Share – meaning...

"Giving a portion of something" to someone/something else.

Show-off – meaning...

"Boastfully display one's ability or accomplishments".

Sharing and showing-off are totally different things; one is positive and inspiring; the other, negative and to be avoided at all costs! So please don't let the worry of being a "show-off" get in the way of you sharing your brilliance!

I used to feel uncomfortable at the thought of sharing my "stuff", feeling exposed and worried that I didn't have good enough material to share. However, I've got over myself! I now know that sharing isn't about just ME, it's about what I offer! And it turns out that what I have to offer is very useful to some people. The key thing is to find those people who will appreciate what you have to offer!

When you think of the word SHARE, your mind may go towards... that dreaded thought... SOCIAL MEDIA!

This is not simply a marketing book, or guide to social media, "How to get likes and shares". I'm talking about helping you share yourself with the audiences who matter to you and building the confidence and the tools you need to help you strut your stuff in a completely POSITIVE & GENEROUS way. Yes, my intention is to help you take the lid off yourself, stop holding yourself back and unleash you to the world. This is about how you feel about yourself and how you are going to grow as a person in the process – not just about getting shares on social!

Sharing can be Life-Changing.

My Story

A few years ago I ran a "Speak Like a Leader" program for the Nelson Mandela project in the US for young African leaders. At first, the young, talented and enthusiastic group sat conservatively waiting for my BBC broadcasting tips on how to be more visible and speak well (with a clipped British accent!). However, my message wasn't just about being able to stand and speak perfectly, it was about sharing; passion, vision, stories and letting their true feelings come out. It was extraordinary to watch them change from being "la-di-da" polite and data-driven, to life-changing-passionate-roller-coaster performers. When they started to SHARE their true feelings and vision about climate change, providing water to millions of children and health programs across Southern Saharan Africa, I couldn't hold the tears back. Ultimately, I was there to help them change hearts and minds, and they did. They realised that by being Visibly Brilliant (versus quiet and polite) and sharing stories, passion and vision, they felt empowered to take on challenges and make a real change to potentially millions of lives.

Sharing is not selfish!

Striving for Visible Brilliance isn't selfish – it's generous. If you are Visibly Brilliant, you are in a positive position to teach, enable others, empower people, share knowledge, lead with purpose and make an impact!

Being Visibly Brilliant allows you to be a role model. By sharing generously, even your struggles and insecurities, you are helping people, as they will feel they are not alone. You don't have to be perfect and have three PhDs in order to share. It's not just clever content and lots of knowledge you need to share (another misconception); it's your stories and experiences – and these can be simple ideas, concepts, feelings, and relatable observations.

There's one magic word here that sums up your strategy to discover your Visible Brilliance. That word is simply...

SHARE

From now on (and for the rest of your life), you need to share your brilliant self, MORE.

Don't worry, you don't need to overshare! But be brave, you do have to get out there and lay yourself bare! Yikes, it sounds a bit daunting, but it doesn't have to be. You can do this!!

What do I mean by share yourself?

My good friend, Jacq, tells me her experience of not being Visibly Brilliant (unlike her sister) has taught her how valuable sharing herself with the outside world is.

"A while ago, my sister and I worked at the same high-profile publishing house in London.

She knew if she focused on the numbers and was outspoken about the bottom line and the revenue of the business, she'd be seen as Visibly Brilliant. Within months of working there, the CEO knew who she was, and they were on corridor-chatting terms. She put herself in the position where she was recognised internally for her entrepreneurial spirit.

I don't think the CEO ever really knew who I was, even though I was publishing bestsellers on a regular basis. My boss at the time claimed the success of all my bestsellers as hers. Therefore, I realised, Visible Brilliance can be as little as just fulfilling the job requirements, hitting the targets and making damn sure people know about it. You don't need to slog your guts out and work more hours than anyone else. I realise now, I was grinding away and not being recognised for my brilliance."

To be Visibly Brilliant, you'll need to be brave and share your achievements as well as all these great qualities:

- Knowledge
- Expertise
- Experience
- Personality
- Stories
- Love
- Insights
- Vision
- Humour
- Everything worth sharing

When it comes to sharing yourself and revealing yourself to the outside world, you can feel vulnerable. There are parts of you that you'd rather keep under wraps, yes absolutely. That's ok, it's normal to feel like you want to keep yourself safe. However, sharing "a portion" of you is essential to being Visibly Brilliant. In fact, it's KEY. Don't worry, we are going to focus on the positives, the GIVING part of sharing, allowing people to understand the value you bring and help them learn from you as a leader, that is generous, positive and life-changing for you and the people you are going to help or lead.

You need to be prepared to be brave and share (within reason – you don't need to talk about your divorce and EVERY SINGLE innermost thought!). However, the more you are prepared to share your true self and your experiences, the more your audiences (and I mean any audience here; boss, clients or colleagues in the coffee meeting) will trust you, love you and want to go on a journey with you.

Does the thought of sharing make you feel naked?

Ask yourself...

- Who am I?
- What do I stand for?
- What's my mission?
- Why does it matter?
- What's my vibe?
- Who cares?

I find many of my clients who step into leadership roles don't feel the FREEDOM to be themselves or know themselves. They often try to imitate others or please other people. It takes time and focus and quite a lot of soul-searching to find that freedom. But when you find it, WOW, it's awesome. You no longer feel like you're struggling with your imposter syndrome or FOPO (fear of other people's opinions) because you've found your way.

Then you can go from technically brilliant to Visibly Brilliant!

SHOW NOT TELL

The big mistake many of my clients make, many of whom are leaders, is to work hard and achieve what they THINK others need them to do. They try to live up to an expectation set by someone else; their organisation, their boss, their own team or clients. They don't realise that they can create their own unique and wonderful Visibly Brilliant expectation.

Being successful requires you to focus on the RIGHT path for you and you alone – it's no good trying to follow someone else's Visibly Brilliant journey. They are not the same as you.

My Story

When I first started writing this book, I wasn't 100% sure how it was going to pan out. I knew I wanted to share my pearls of wisdom and 30-plus years of experience with you about my own struggles with confidence, the courage to leave the BBC, set up my own business and venture onto that Visibly Brilliant track. However, when I started the process, I realised I didn't have an obvious and smooth path. There were elements of my content about confidence and getting myself out there that didn't quite fit. I felt like I was trying to please the brilliant Jacq Burns (my literary agent and expert author), and I wasn't being true to myself. When she'd give me feedback, I'd crumble and feel a whole lot of self-doubt flooding in. I tried to figure out a good brainstorming method, ended up with hundreds of Post-it notes all over the place and felt like a crazy person! I realise now, I hadn't found my own path; I was trying to shoehorn things in that didn't fit and re-version blogs that had the wrong tone, and I was all at sea.

I'm sure you've felt that about your own business or career, all at sea with the sails of your ship flapping around with no fixed destination to head for. Maybe you've set unrealistic goals for yourself that are too overwhelming to commit to, so you get side-tracked with something shiny "over there", or easy and achievable "over here", to keep you busy. At least you feel useful when you're doing something easy to keep you occupied, right? Yes, I do that all the time!

Don't worry, you are going to figure out how you are going to navigate your way to your chosen Visibly Brilliant destination. Perhaps that destination will change and evolve over time; after all, your Visible Brilliance is never "finished."

I'm still figuring out my path and I've reached what some people might think is fully blown Visible Brilliance. I'm a prime procrastinator when I am overwhelmed or venture outside my comfort zone. Don't worry, that's normal, but I have also learnt to live with the feeling of discomfort to go ahead and share my content anyway. I've learnt to accept that I might feel shame that I am not perfect, or my material might not be 100% perfect every time.

It's very easy to get side-tracked with figuring out how you're going to come up with YOUR own Visibly Brilliant strategy. You may hear pieces of random advice or pearls of wisdom from people more senior than you, such as, "**You must wear red in meetings to stand out".** It's easy to take advice from others and think you have to do what they do in order to be successful. Yes, it is a good idea to wear a colour that suits you to stand out, but beware the random "be more visible" hacks from other people who won't necessarily help you in the longer term. Red may not be your colour – but purple might!

Hey, advice is great. Do consider comments and learn from other people, for sure. For example, in his book "The 7 Habits of Highly Effective People", Stephen R. Covey has some extremely useful practices that are worth adopting like "be proactive". However, the formula to your personal Visible Brilliance is NOT going to be the same as Stephen or anyone else! You can pick and choose which habits you take on, or even set your own rules and pioneer your own path!

That's what this book is about – getting YOUR ducks in a row and preparing yourself to share your "stuff"…

- To the right people
- With the right content
- At the right time
  And
- Doing it really well!

And it's got to be in the right way that fits you:

- Your type
- Your path
- Your vision
- Your personality

And when you have all these things figured out – when you share and are booked to speak on panels, at the town hall meeting or at a conference, if you get all these things right, you will be asked again and again. That's the beauty of getting your Visibly Brilliant toolkit in order – it's incredibly efficient and it works for ALL occasions.

SHARE YOUR FEELINGS

Before you know it, you'll be invited to write a guest article, to be interviewed on a podcast, or even write a book. It's incredible how quickly and efficiently you can speed up the Visibly Brilliant process if you know what to do and how to do it. And the good news is it doesn't have to be painful with that constant worry of feeling judged.

2 TIPS

Talented TIP – *You have talent, so share it! Share your best bits, insights, knowledge, experience, stories – you will feel useful... and you won't feel like a show-off!*

Therapeutic TIP – *Think about how you could help others by being brave and sharing your thoughts and feelings with the outside world. Sometimes, sharing your insecurities helps others relate to you more – they will appreciate your honesty.*

★★★★★★★★★★★★★★★★★★★★★★★★★★

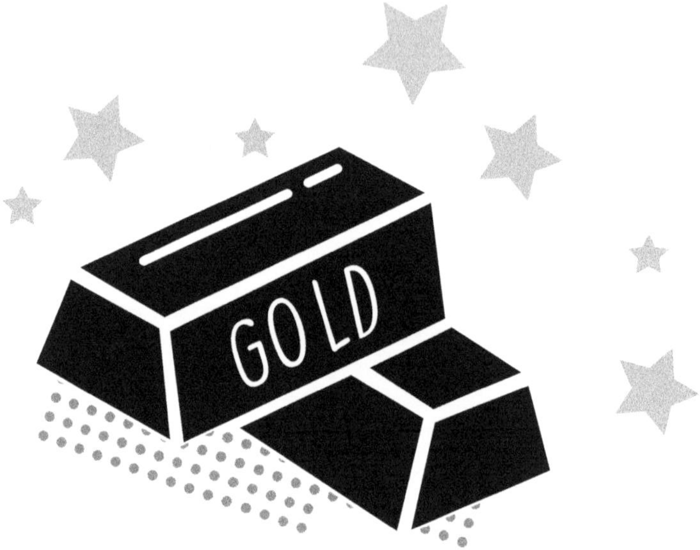
GOLD

CHAPTER 23

HOW TO SHARE YOUR STUFF!

★★★★★★★★★★★★★★★★★★★★★★★★★★

How to dig for content gold? "What is that?" you ask. It's your "stuff", your ideas, thoughts, vision, stories and insights. And guess what? Your content doesn't have to be the biggest thought or insight since Aristotle, Einstein or Maya Angelou, no, no, no! I'm going to show you how sharing doesn't require as much research, worry or prep as you think. So don't overthink this, I've got your back.

How? That's where the Triple A formula comes in – that's coming up shortly. It is the formula to enable you to craft killer content, your way, your style, your "type" for your unique audiences (i.e. the people who matter to you the most). I call it "Content Gold." More on that later. Before we dig for that content gold, let's talk about SHARING.

A quick reminder here. Sharing yourself is NOT the same as showing off. Sharing is generous, and the more you share, the more visible you are going to be.

If you've ever been on a social media course, you'll know the good sharers are the successful social media influencers. However, don't let social media or the thought of having to post on multiple platforms distract you from your Visibly Brilliant quest. Social media might be an obvious first step to being visible, and we will be venturing into that murky world, but it's not the be all and end all. Being Visibly Brilliant is about sharing yourself on a much deeper level.

This is NOT a social media book.

It is much more than that. It's about how you feel about yourself and how you build your inner confidence, so you shine on the outside, whether it's online, in person, in a meeting or on a podcast.

Leaders share their thoughts and feelings, on many platforms in many ways, because sharing is the secret sauce to being seen as a "thought leader" or, in simple terms, the "I know my sh*t" person! People with a high status, confident enough to lay themselves bare, warts and all. The ones willing to tell the truth about themselves and their knowledge are the leaders and winners when it comes to being more visible. If you're not willing to "go there" and share, but resort to the same old generic stuff that everyone else says, you'll not reach your Visibly Brilliant goal and stand out from the crowd.

Yes, you may feel exposed and naked. Here's a funny thing. When you think about public speaking, one of my areas of expertise, people often suggest that you imagine the audience naked! (By the way, it doesn't work, it just distracts!) When I used to think about being Visibly Brilliant, I used to feel as if I was naked (not the audience!) and the whole audience was looking up and pointing at me with my droopy bits! However, I've overcome my naked fears, and I can say with hand on heart, you will feel comfortable in front of the most difficult audiences and able to "bare all" if you stick to your guns and prepare yourself for it. Seriously, you've got this, oh naked one!

It's down to YOU and only you.

You are in control of your own Visibly Brilliant destiny. One option is to ask for help – it's a good idea, I get help all the time. You may have people who can post and publish your content for you; however, YOU have to drive your own Visibly Brilliant strategy.

It can take a bit of time, but, if you do just one thing a day, and I suggest you spend just 10-15 minutes a day focusing on this, you will soon reach that peak. Just like climbing a mountain. One step at a time – one step, it doesn't matter what you do, just do SOMETHING.

That one thing a day leads to five to seven in a week (depending on days off!). Anything is better than zero – tumbleweed.

Taking a bit of time isn't a bad thing though as it gives you time to get used to it. That shudder when you post your first article, or that first presentation to the management that feels totally out of your comfort zone. However, when you've done it three or four times, it starts to feel normal. I often find, if you do something seven times, the fear fades!

Aren't we just talking "Personal Brand"?

It's all about perception. What we're talking about here is your personal brand, yes. And what I mean by "personal brand" is simply the way you come across to other people.

When you show up, people will look at you and make a judgement as to if/why you are worth listening to. That's life, nothing to be afraid of. It's what we are all programmed to do; to make a quick assessment about the person in front of us. So why not flex your Visibly Brilliant muscles and prepare for the best version of you to walk through that door, onto that stage or into that meeting room?

Your audience will sniff you out if you are not sharing "properly" in an authentic Visibly Brilliant way. If you are being your authentic version of Visibly Brilliant, you're being true to yourself.

> **True to Life TIP** – *When you are being truthful about you, telling true stories about yourself and sharing your true self, you are much more likely to connect and attract people to you, as they will find you more engaging.*

Practical tips on how to share...

Let's get practical. Take your pen and notebook out or use the notes pages at the back of the book... and start thinking about these questions...

- *How do you share yourself?*
- *How do you choose what to share?*
- *What is Content Gold?*
- *Who do you share it with?*
- *Where do you share it?*
- *Why do you share it?*
- *What's the benefit?*
- *Will it ever feel comfortable? (Yes, don't worry, it will!)*

These are the steps to sharing... I talk about this in my TEDx talk...

S SPEAK

O OPPORTUNITIES

W WRITE

SOW – SPEAK

Hey, I used to be terrified of public speaking, hence my first book "Goodbye Glossophobia: banish your fear of public speaking." I used to be nervous, and shake and sweat as soon as I felt the spotlight on me. My mind used to go blank. However, I cured myself by doing it again and again and again. Please don't let public speaking nerves put you off. You can start by simply speaking in front of small groups, maybe your team meeting or an awayday. The main tip here is to keep doing it – even if you don't LOVE it at first, the more you do, the more you WILL be comfortable in the spotlight.

When you are the person at the front of the room sharing your knowledge, it's a gamechanger to you, your confidence and the way people see you. And you WILL get over your nerves the more you do.

My big ask of you is this: Get yourself a gig once a week if you can. "But Where? When? How?" you ask.

Hey, any opportunity: a meeting, a "best practice" training session, your old school, a podcast, an internal vlog, a video update, an awayday or even a conference. Please don't shy away from putting yourself forward as the expert, host or presenter. Do it and you will get used to it. I have loads of tips on how to craft your material. You CAN do this. Start small.

SOW – OPPORTUNITY

If you don't find opportunities to speak and you don't get invited to speak at conferences or your AGM (Annual General Meeting), then DON'T WAIT, CREATE. Here's how my client Celine transformed from silent and invisible to the go-to spokesperson in her organisation.

Celine was terrified of public speaking. She was one of "The Invisibles" in her organisation. She worked in a customer facing role in a bank and worked harder than everyone else and was super-bright. Yet, she didn't get promoted one year when her close colleague did! She was devastated.

When I worked with her one-to-one, she was resentful about having to "put herself out there". She hated LinkedIn and complained that she didn't want to "play the game" – in her mind, she felt she had to "pretend" to be confident on the outside and didn't feel comfortable with the whole self-promotion thing.

I explained that if she was invisible, it made her less likely to be recognised and rewarded for all her hard work.

She wasn't used to speaking or hosting and had avoided it up until she met me, because she was "busy" doing her day job, and felt promoting herself was selfish. However, after her disappointment of being overlooked, she realised she had to do something about her Visibility – FAST.

So, we cooked up a plan. She was already a committee member on the Diversity Network; however, she wasn't very active and didn't get involved that much. We decided to create a breakfast networking event that she could host. She invited a couple of charismatic colleagues to share their stories, and she planned to introduce the event and ask questions. Success! All she had to do was introduce the event, literally two minutes of welcoming the audience and introducing her guests. It was brilliant! After the first event, everyone wanted more, so it became a monthly thing. Plus, other people in the audience saw that she was the person speaking at the front, so they stared asking her to do other events, internal at first. Because of these regular events, she got used to the sensation of standing in front of an audience, and asking questions and started to ENJOY IT!

Now she is the go-to spokesperson when it comes to diversity in her organisation. She is well known, she had a "Spotlight" article written about her in one of the industry magazines, she is championed in the boardroom... they know who she is, and she is celebrated.

The lesson here is: all that work that seems "extra" to your day job is worth it. It's worth building your profile for the long term, as you will get recognised the more you put yourself out there. Start small, remember – seek out opportunities to speak, share, host, moderate a panel or speak at a conference.

SOW – WRITE

I NEVER in my wildest dreams thought I'd be able to write anything "professional". Doing my "Friday Tips" newsletter didn't come naturally and my first book "Goodbye Glossophobia: Banish your fear of public speaking" won a Highly Commended Business Book of the Year Award! Woo-hoo!

What I know NOW is this: Writing isn't about writing things down; writing is about expressing yourself. It's about having somewhere to dump your ideas, dump your stuff. You really don't need to be a "writer" to write. In fact, AI has changed the way everyone approaches writing. You can speak gobble-de-gook into ChatGPT, and it can give you a fantastic chunk of written content. So now we know writing doesn't have to be intimidating or perfect, it's time to get into the habit of writing down your thoughts, ideas, vision for the future, stories, experiences, lessons learnt... ooh there's so much great stuff you can jot down and share.

Here's the thing. If you write your "stuff" down and you have somewhere to park your thoughts, inspiration, knowledge, insights, feelings and ideas, you'll create your own hot bed of content ready to share. The key thing is to start the habit now!

And if you're thinking, "I don't usually have all these things bubbling around in my head and I have ZERO inspiration to write anything...", then don't worry, I'll help you! Please read on!

You can start by using the notes at the back of this book... all you need to do is this one thing today... So just START – even a small scribble. Begin by merely writing down what's on your mind right now.

Or try this mini exercise...

GET CRACKING

Let's have a little play...

You can use your notebook or the pages at the back of this book if you like. Have a go at answering these questions using SOW.

1. Speak – Where could you speak? Meetings, AGMs, off-sites, awaydays, best practice sessions, conferences?

2. Opportunities – What could you create, like Celine and her diversity networking event? It doesn't have to be big; it can be a five-minute slot as part of something else.

3. Write – This is a fun one! Use the notes at the back of this book to write about one piece of knowledge you could share about what you do... could be a project, a leadership tip, dealing with difficult problems, or difficult people! Choose one thing that pops into your head and try this method that I call...

The BOWIE method!

So yes, I created this easy writing hack to help you put pen to paper.

Often, if you have to write something – an article, blog, post, presentation script or even a chapter for your next book – it's easier to have a system rather than an intimidating blank sheet of paper or computer screen.

Try this. First, choose a simple topic. Pick a subject you've been talking about recently; you may have had the urge to write or post about this on LinkedIn. NO pressure – you don't need to post this; it's just a starting point. For example, it could be a plan for a project for later this year, or a little story about a successful project or achievement you accomplished recently, or something you learnt from your latest staff awayday. It could even be a charity bike ride. Don't overthink. Just choose ONE topic or subject, and let's put the BOWIE method to the test.

GRAB A PEN

Use your notebook or turn to the back of the book and try this easy writing exercise.

BRAIN DUMP
Empty your head of ideas, no matter how silly, creative, dumb... just get them onto the page.

ORDER
Put your material into a rough order; beginning, middle, end.

WRITE
You only write once you've got ideas in front of you in a rough order.

INSTINCT
Let your instincts take your writing to its natural conclusion but still without a filter or any editing.

EDIT
Now you, the editor, is allowed into the room. The spelling, grammar and shaping police!

Let's get into the detail now:

B – Brain dump! First of all, with NO filter, write down all the possible things you can think of around your chosen topic. So, for example, if you did a psychometric test on your last awayday and you came out as an Introvert... then perhaps you could write about it.

You may have:
- Evidence or data to share (for example, your Myers Briggs or Insights profile)
- Maybe you have a childhood story or recent story that backs this up
- Perhaps you've had feedback or comments from others about it
- Other observations from your past, present or future
- Any other stuff you think might be relevant to this topic

The beauty of this method is **YOU ARE FREE** to write whatever you like for this step. Don't be tempted to start fiddling with spelling and grammar... yet. That will come later. Trust me, write like no one's watching for your brain dump. No judgement, no rules, it doesn't have to be brilliant.

O – Order. Put your material into a rough order; beginning, middle, end. So, your top line (beginning) could be, "I've always been introvert." Then you may have a story, "I remember one time when..." – this is your (middle) – and that story may have elements you could bring in. Then perhaps you have some lessons learnt or some stats to add. At the end, you may have a conclusion (the ending) that brings you full circle "What I've learnt is to work with my type". Or you may end on tips or an action point. I often end my blogs or posts on a "Get in touch" or "Click here" action. There's no right or wrong.

W – Write. Yes, that's correct! You only write once you've got ideas in front of you. Now you can fill in the gaps and actually start "writing" the piece. I personally find this so much easier when I've already thought through the ideas, the rough order and I've digested what I might have as my message or action point. Take your time, don't try and be perfect; this is only step three of the process.

I – Instinct. Let your instincts take your writing to its natural conclusion but still with no filter. I'm adding in this step because sometimes it helps to take a step back, even a little break, and go with the flow; no rules, regulations, no "Shouldn't I write this?". This is to remind you to feel the words as you write, let your fingers do the talking. Add feelings, emotions, similes and metaphors into your sentences. When you are going with the flow, writing becomes easy, like a knife through butter!

If you're not used to writing, you may need to trick yourself into imagining you are a bestselling author... and write "as if" you are totally comfortable.

And finally,

E – Edit. Now you, yes, you, are now the editor. Now you are allowed into the room as the spelling, grammar and shaping police. This is where you take a step back, even come back the next day, and edit, tweak, enhance, use fancy words, use AI if you like...

NOW you finish the post off with flair, grammar and punchy one-line paragraphs.

If you ask AI for help and ask to "Please punch this up and make it shorter" then great. However, make sure you edit your AI version to suit your own style.

Please make a note of BOWIE and use it next time you are creating content. It is a brilliant tool!

NOTES

The most important thing is that you are writing down your "stuff". You can use this material for any occasion in the future.

> **Thoroughly Freeing TIP –** *When you write, make sure your inner editor isn't in the room at the same time as your inner writer. Let yourself go, be free, with no filters when you get going. Only when you have allowed yourself permission to express yourself, warts and all, on paper... then, and only then, you can start the editing process.*

OMG

This tip has changed my life!

If you let your editor in at the same time as your writer, you're likely to get WRITER'S BLOCK! I don't get that anymore because I allow my "unedited' self to jot down the rough ideas on paper first. I now feel FREE to express myself.

★★★★★★★★★★★★★★★★★★★★★★★★★

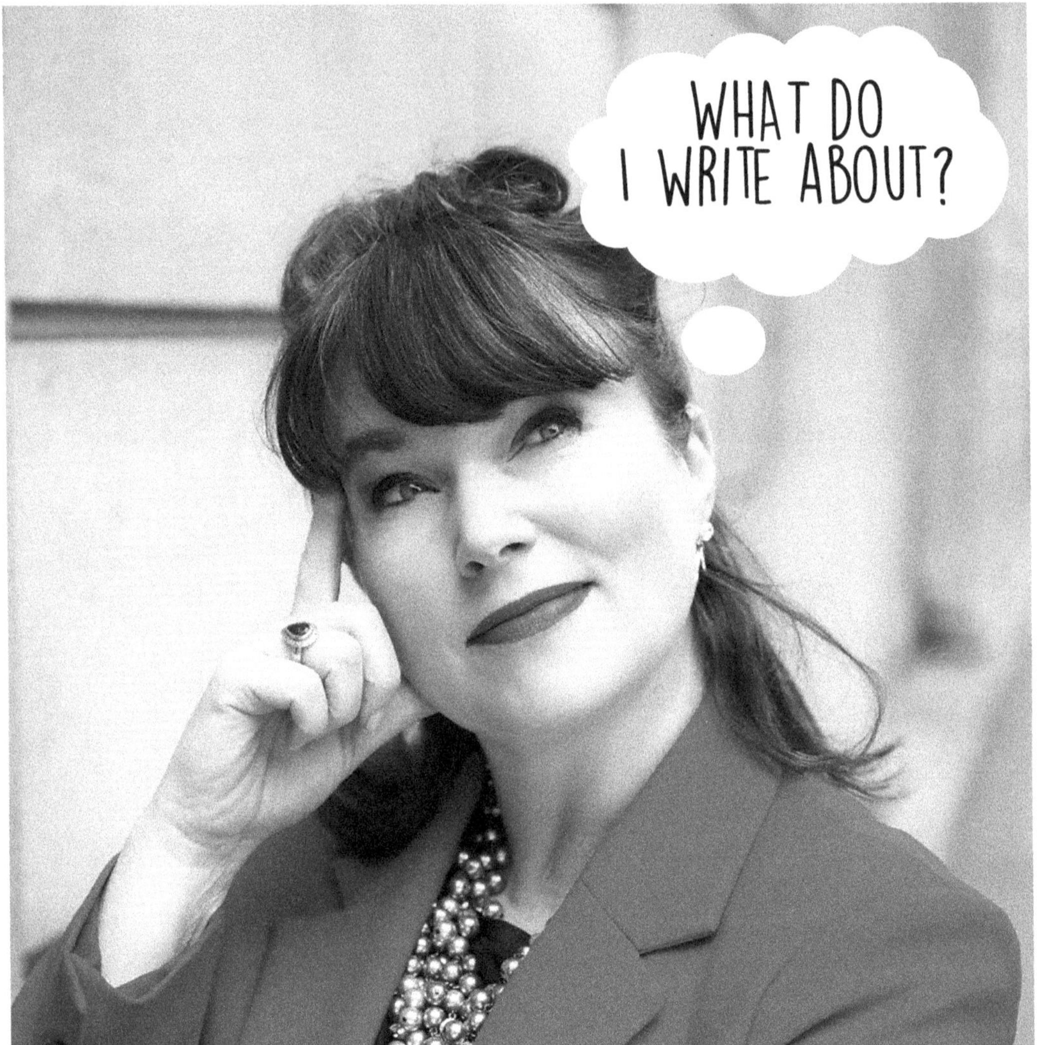
WHAT DO
I WRITE ABOUT?

CHAPTER 24

DIGGING FOR CONTENT GOLD

★★★★★★★★★★★★★★★★★★★★★★★★★

When I started The Impact Guru business and my quest for Visible Brilliance, I used to panic at the thought of having to share content, both written and spoken. I used to think the following:

- What do I write about? My mind's gone blank!
- What am I going to talk about?
- I'm not a natural at presenting
- I'm not very interesting – why would anyone want to hear my boring stuff!
- I'm not articulate

Do you relate to this? Well, I can safely say boll**ks to that (that's a rude word).

You ARE interesting because you have lived a life, lead a team, worked in organisations, been brought up with siblings, no siblings, travelled, experienced hopes, fears and learnt a great deal about... LIFE! You LIVE A LIFE and therefore you ARE interesting. So there`– no excuses!

Let's get digging.

Grab a pen and your journal or use the pages at the back of the book. Let's dive into your "stuff"!

<u>YOUR KNOWLEDGE</u>

<u>YOUR EXPERTISE</u>

<u>YOUR EXPERIENCE</u>

And this is just the TOTI – tip of the iceberg! Let's get stuck in!

KNOWLEDGE – You KNOW stuff!

Exercise: What do YOU know, and others don't?

Whatever your background or sector, you have unique knowledge. For example, my knowledge and experience working with leaders who dread public speaking means that I have many stories, insights and scientific research to share about nerves, glossophobia (fear of public speaking) and stepping into the spotlight. When I work with clients and they tell me how they feel about their inner confidence levels and what's really going on behind the scenes, this creates brilliant case studies and real-life examples that people can relate to. The trick is to share "useful" content that will help people.

EXPERTISE – You ARE the expert!

Exercise: What is YOUR expertise?

There's no right or wrong! Think of your top three tips you can share, no matter what your field. For example, if you are a data analyst, you will have three tips you could share that help you do your job more efficiently. If you are a female leader in the army, you have many tips and tricks you've picked up from your role. If you're in publishing, you KNOW what makes a good proposal, and so on.

EXPERIENCE – you have LOADS.

Exercise: Think of a light bulb moment, a memory, or a time when you made a huge mistake and learnt a lesson?

OMG, the stories are endless. I will help you dig deeper and discover more stories later too.

> **Thrilling TIP –** *When telling a story, simply share a memory and start with the following sentence*
>
> *"I remember when..."*

★★★★★★★★★★★★★★★★★★★★★★★★★

22

WHAT'S THE STORY

CHAPTER 25

STORYTELLING

★★★★★★★★★★★★★★★★★★★★★★★★★

Stories fuel your Visible Brilliance. Here's some inspiration to help you find yours.

Cognitive psychologist Jerome Bruner (1915-2016) suggests we are 22 times more likely to remember a fact when it is presented as a story. Why? Because stories are memorable, and usually trigger our emotions.

Get cracking and have a go at this practical exercise:

Find one story that describes the kind of person you are – you have hundreds. The trick is to use my "chunkology" strategy of one at a time! Start with childhood – what were you good at? When were you praised? How does this relate to what you do now?

FIRSTS

Think of firsts: "The first time I... worked, realised I was good at (add what you want in here), found out I was going to college, passed an exam, travelled, moved jobs, fell in love..." The list goes on because there are stories **everywhere.**

WORSTS

Then do the same for **Worsts!** The worst boss you ever had, the worst job (mine was helping my brother with his paper round – we had to deliver newspapers to these horrid blocks of flats in West London; it was smelly and scary!).

LOVE

What do you LOVE? From spreadsheets to writing or running for charity. What you love and are passionate about is the perfect thing to share. You are giving part of yourself away to others. It's generous, not selfish. You can talk about the people you love if it's relevant to the audience. I love helping people to speak in public even if they are scared at first... I love it when they say, *"I nailed it!"*

INSIGHTS

Lessons learnt, observations from your work and life, professional lessons learnt – you have loads. Jot some down!

VISION

Ideas for the future: what would make your organisation better? What about AI and technology? What could you do to change and improve efficiency? I bet you have hundreds of ideas up your sleeve. Start making notes on all your lovely conversations you have at the bar after work or with your partner or family.

HUMOUR

Yes, you DO have a sense of humour! Listen to this tip: in all your sharing, DO remember that you are a human being, and you are FUN. Find the fun. Stop being so earnest!

OBSERVATIONS ABOUT YOUR LIFE AND WORK

Anything goes. Most things you have to say are interesting to a certain audience. Your observations are unique to you; AI can't make them up. I bet you can think of a few "obs" about your job, your clients and colleagues! I bet your observations could help someone somewhere feel like they are not alone, or you may be able to help by sharing your wisdom.

EASY STORY FINDERS

Need inspiration to find a good story? One of my clients asked me how I find good stories in work and in life and I sent her this list of triggers which she found incredibly helpful. See if you can create stories out of these...

Here are my top 10 easy story-finder triggers...

1. **Firsts:** "The first time I met the boss…"
2. **Worsts:** "The worst job I ever had…"
3. **When I was studying:** "… for my engineering degree, I was the best in class for xxx" (might be an insight into your background)
4. **Childhood:** "When I was 6 I used to save up all my pennies…" (could be a character trait)
5. **Why this role?:** "The thing that most inspired me to move to Ruth's team was…"
6. **Best Project Ever:** "In 2019 we had the biggest challenge we'd ever faced…"
7. **Lessons Learnt:** "In 2024 I had an uphill struggle… with the ESG project…"
8. **Role Models:** "The women who have inspired me in my life are…" (stories for each woman)
9. **FAQs:** The most frequently asked question e.g. "What's the main issue with your ESG team?"
10. **Awards!** "In 2025 our team won the award for xxx. It was such a fantastic moment for me personally because xxx"

TERRIFIC TIP – *Remember that stories are 22 times more memorable than facts alone! Go on, I dare you. Jot one down today!*

★★★★★★★★★★★★★★★★★★★★★★★★

TRIPLE A FORMULA

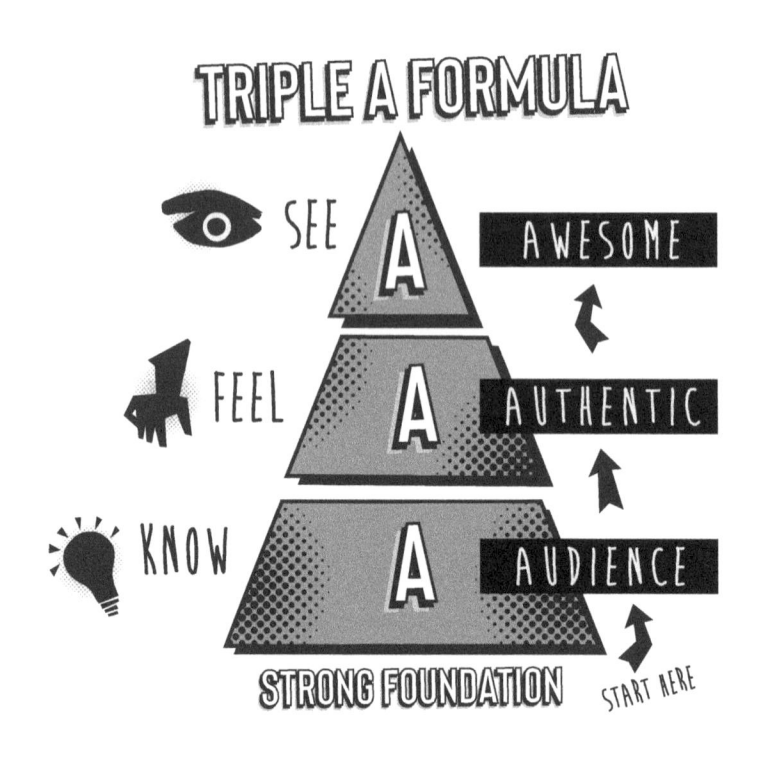

- **SEE** → **A** AWESOME
- **FEEL** → **A** AUTHENTIC
- **KNOW** → **A** AUDIENCE

STRONG FOUNDATION — START HERE

> The Triple A is NOT just a formula for public speaking, presentations or pitches; it's a formula for anytime you want to show up and shine, walk into a room or log onto a Zoom. It's useful for everyday work and life. It can be used to prep content for phone calls, difficult conversations, pitches or writing a simple post!

CHAPTER 26

HOW TO MAKE THIS INTO CONTENT GOLD

★★★★★★★★★★★★★★★★★★★★★★★★★★

From all my years at the BBC and working with business leaders, I've created this easy formula. In my experience, this is foundation to ALL communication. It's where you start when you want to produce a juicy piece of content for any audience at any given time. Let's unwrap it and start at the bottom of the pyramid!

I always work my way through the formula in this order...
(from the bottom up, darling!)

A — AUDIENCE — FOUNDATION

A — AUTHENTIC — YOUR BRILLIANT STORIES AND INSIGHTS

A — AWESOME — LOOK, SOUND, FEEL BRILLIANT

The Triple A formula is designed to help you captivate your audience: any audience (your boss, your clients, your colleagues, or your customers) for any scenario. It is designed to help you be YOU, warts and all; show your hidden talents and personality traits, plus it's designed to help you LOOK, SOUND and FEEL awesome so the world can see how brilliant (and fabulous) you are!

From now on, the Triple A formula will be the foundation to all your content when preparing for writing and "gigs" (i.e. any time you need to speak and come across as credible and confident) from pitches and posts to "seasonal chats" and meetings.

> **Simple TIP** – *To start you off: SMILE (eyes and teeth) will help you to achieve Visible Brilliance!*

DAVE AND SUE

CHAPTER 27

DIVE INTO THE DETAIL OF THE TRIPLE A FORMULA!

★★★★★★★★★★★★★★★★★★★★★★★★★

A A A `AUDIENCE` – YOU ALWAYS START HERE

You can be Visibly Brilliant from your audience's point of view.

For any scenario, get into your audience's head, choose someone that represents the majority and step into their shoes (could be the key decision maker or an "avatar" of a larger audience i.e., someone who represents the majority). At the BBC, our audience used to be "Dave and Sue"!

You need to picture your "avatar", your typical audience member in your mind. Yes, name them, like Dave and Sue; it's best to picture a real person. For example, the other day my client told me all about his audience member "Peter" who was ambitious, wanted an easy life, yet also demanded a good bonus. "Peter" was worried about risk and compliance. It made writing for the "Peter" audience targeted and meaningful.

When you have your audience avatar in your mind, try and become them for a few moments. Role play and write down what you (they) are really thinking about, what you (they) care about, and what you (they) NEED at that moment at that time. It might be something simple like "When's lunch?" or "I hope this is interesting," or "Will I make more money out of this?"

Once you've accepted and digested what your "audience" really, really needs, then you can create Content Gold. It almost starts writing itself!

My one tip, which the former Prime Minister Boris Johnson asked me to share with him when I was producing shows at the BBC, was the most valuable tip of ALL:

"Boris, all you have to do is love your audience a little bit more than yourself!"

Not sure he took my advice (!) but you can. Serve them FIRST, before you serve yourself. This applies to ALL of your content.

Start with a blank page and fill it with what I call my ***"Audience Audit"***.

Quick fix – step into their shoes and ask *'What's in it for me? WIIFM"*

> **Truthful TIP** – *They don't care about you; they only care about themselves (not in a bad way, they are only human!)*

AAA AUTHENTIC – IN OTHER WORDS, BE YOURSELF!

The Triple A is designed to give you a short cut into your "personal brand" (yes, that buzzword!), yet it is so much more than that. Knowing yourself helps you to serve your audience and so they buy into you as a person.

You can tell when someone isn't being themselves, can't you? It's a real turn-off when you feel someone isn't being genuine or owning their own space.

Celebrate your best bits, who you are, where you are from, the languages you speak and your authentic personality, the whole lot! You can be Visibly Brilliant from the inside out! Your inner brilliance can shine out if you let it.

Being yourself – your TRUE self – is the key to creating content gold; it's truthful, real, and makes people FEEL something because you are more relatable when you're being human. Your unique lived experiences can't be replicated by AI. Simply by telling your own stories, your truth, from your point of view and sharing your insights, will help you write and share great content more easily.

> **Touchy-Feely TIP 1** – *Be open minded; learn about yourself, embrace self-development. It's changed my life. It's fun to discover your personality traits, "natural" preferences and type. I'm an extreme extrovert and married to an introvert!*

I'm also going to urge you to think about sharing your hidden stories and content from your background; childhood memories, professional highs and lows, lessons learnt, your many 'first" experiences as discussed in Chapter 25 and more juicy stuff you've not shared yet!

> **Touchy-Feely TIP 2** – *Your personal life story will never date; you will be able to use all the lovely material that you have written from your notes from reading this book, forever!*

GET CRACKING

Here's a little "authentic" exercise to get your teeth into

Grab a pen, paper and a person you know, like and trust, such as family, a friend or a colleague! But no "judgy" people please – this isn't a toxic 360-degree feedback!

This is the fun bit. How to figure out the authentic YOU in one go...

It's ok if you find your best bits are also your worst bits – that's normal. They are often two sides of the same coin. Careful not to be too self-critical. I often tell myself off for being "too bubbly"!

Interview your nearest and dearest about YOU; ask them and yourself these four questions and jot the replies down.

1. How would you describe my personality? (Not competencies)

Titillating TIP – *Don't forget the humour!*

> 1. SCRIBBLE HERE...

2. What's my USP? (Unique Selling Point) What's my superpower?

> 2. SCRIBBLE HERE...

3. What am I strangely good at? Such as a party piece? Could be random, like walking on your hands, crosswords, Excel spreadsheets or sailing! (It turns out I can make a very loud clicking noise with my tongue!)

```
3. SCRIBBLE HERE...
```

4. What's my hashtag? LOL, have a go at this. It's great fun! Hey, if you can't figure out a hashtag at first, don't worry – just pick three words to describe YOU, such as Sunny, Driven, Spanish. Put these together to create a hashtag. Venture outside your comfort zone; use colours, even emojis! Be creative, have fun with it. You don't have to use your hashtag on social media – this is merely an exercise to get you thinking about YOU; who you are and the way you roll!

```
4. SCRIBBLE HERE...
```

Here are some examples!

#BROMLEYCHAMELEON   #DATANAUTOFBENGAL   #GALOPIN

#SOCIALBUTTERFLY   #COLOMBIANPROBLEMSOLVER   #HAPPYPARISIAN

#ATTACCANTE   #THEONLYYELLOWINCOMPLIANCE   #IPINTIWORLD

My Story

My ability to chat, be creative and come up with a million ideas is a huge asset to my career as a professional speaker, podcaster, writer, and content producer; however, it's also been the bane of my life.

"The trouble with you, Esther, is you have too many ideas!" an old boss told me once.

**ial*I used to feel self-conscious about my chatty style, and my "over-enthusiastic" delivery.*

Once, I was described at a conference as "a fizzy bubble waiting to burst" when I walked onto the stage and started to speak in London. I now take this as a huge compliment! I now use it to celebrate who I am and what I stand for.

I used to hate the "fizzy bubble" part of me, but then I realised it WAS me, my style, and it's just the way I roll. I can't help being the one with "too much energy"!

The lesson? Don't beat yourself up if you keep gravitating towards the negatives. You'll find you can turn them around into a positive or unique personality trait.

Own it!

A client of mine from Italy, Antonio, told me that people thought him "too laid back… and lacking in energy."

He was also dead pan (unlike your archetypal Italian), his humour was very subtle, he didn't smile very much and he could be quite sarcastic. In his professional capacity, he'd hide his humour. SO, as a result he'd be deadpan, not fun at all, and quite frankly rather dull. Yet, he wasn't DULL when he was being himself; he was wonderfully witty, creative, and surprising.

He had a hidden warmth, but he didn't know how to show it. My advice to him? Let it out, show the fun side. Have more fun with ALL your communication, yes, even the quarterly figures! The trick here is to know thyself. Know what type of communicator you are. Don't hide your personality in fear of being unprofessional. Being a professional doesn't mean NO HUMOUR!

Celebrate your TYPE!

Yes, now we're on this authentic path of righteousness… do you know your type?

Now I'm not just talking about psychometric testing. I'm inviting you to know roughly what "type" of person you are… your broad preferences.

Let's take how you approach presentations for example. In my experience as a speech coach for leaders, I find there are two types of "presenters" when it comes to pitching, speaking (with slides), doing a keynote, chairing a panel or being a live 'guest'…

Type 1 – The Plannerina

Type 2 – The Wing-It-Wonder

Which one do you identify with?

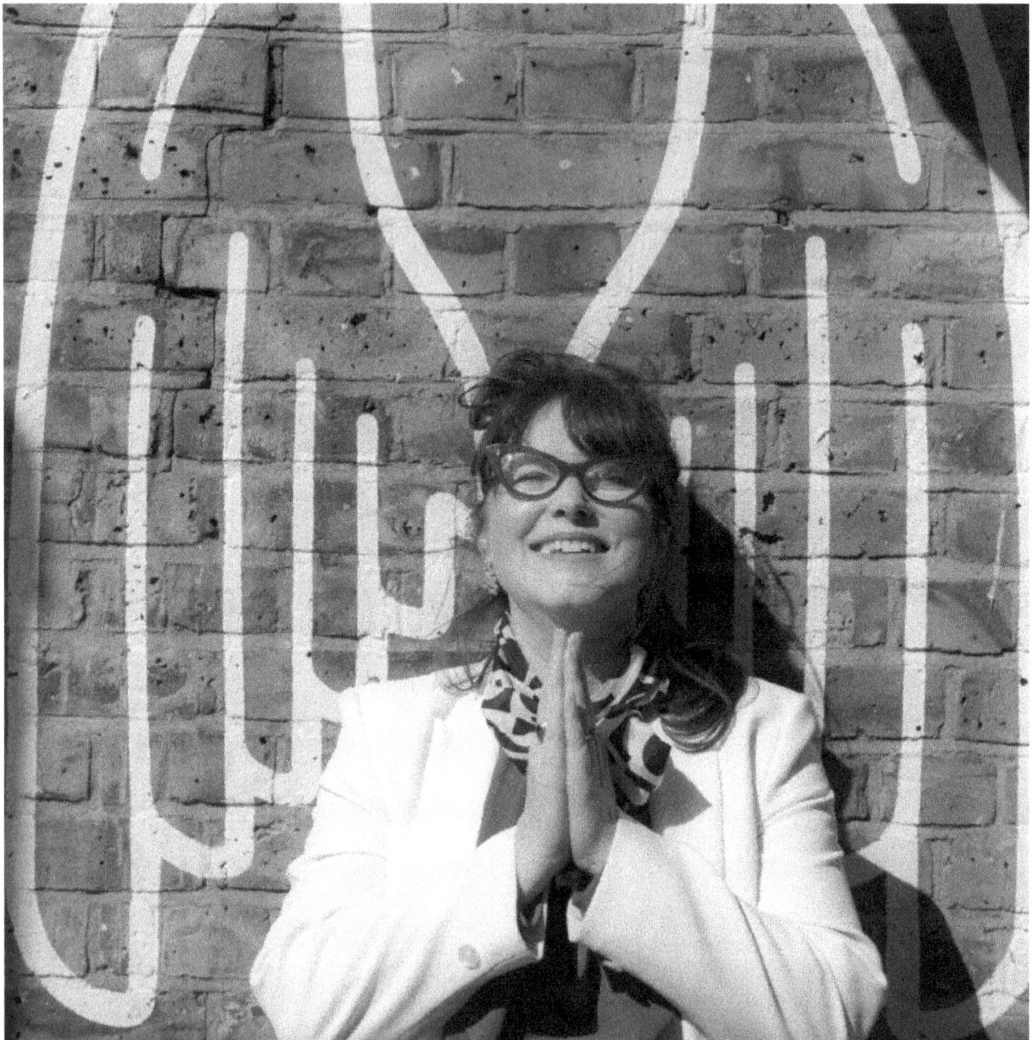

I am probably a Wing-It-Wonder! In other words, "quick & dirty."

Which one are you? Or maybe you're a bit of both.

In my experience (and I've clocked up around 8,000 examples from city clients over the years!), you usually fit into one of these camps.

When I was producing live shows at the BBC, I used to think of Boris Johnson (then Mayor of London) as the pin up 'Wing-It-Wonder' and the former British Prime Minister Theresa May (solid, stable, and secure) as the archetypal Plannerina.

The truth is you do need to PLAN your content, whatever your type. The most important thing is to embrace your natural go-to type and don't try and be like someone else.

Plannerina or Wing-It-Wonder… there's no right or wrong, there's your "natural preference".

> **TIP – For "Plannerinas" – PLAN WIGGLE ROOM!**
> *If you are a Plannerina, learn to flex; it's fine to have a script, it's brilliant to plan … however, you MUST remember what your audience needs at that moment at that time. You need to serve them first, remember?*
>
> **TIP – For "Wing-It-Wonders" – PLAN A ROUGH STUCTURE**
> *or "running order" of chunks. You can ad lib and play inside your structure.*

And if you're a Wing-It-Wonder type, plan a rough structure so you create healthy boundaries for yourself, otherwise you WILL go off track. Sometimes this urge to ad lib can leave the audience confused and even irritated that you digress from your point.

> **TIP – For ALL:** *Celebrate who you are; your personality, culture, type, humour, style, core values... ALL OF YOU. You know when you're being the authentic "you"; it takes courage (and practice) to show up and be YOU.*

There's no right or wrong, and there are thousands of ways to share your message. However, when you're being true to yourself, you're in flow and you give the audience what they need... you can feel in your gut, you're on the right track for YOU!

A A A AWESOME

Yes. You can be Visibly Brilliant from the outside. The way you look and sound on a surface level is powerful!

Being awesome is much easier than you think, even if you don't FEEL it inside. My quick fix P.O.S.E. formula can transform you in a matter of seconds. I created "P.O.S.E." at the BBC to help nervous guests become brilliant live on air in a matter of minutes and it still works a treat for ANY OCCASION. Try this:

POSE — P IS FOR POSTURE —

Think BIG, shoulders back, head up. The yoga Tadasana (Mountain) pose is a useful place to start. Plant your feet so you have a solid base, stretch your spine out and imagine your head is being pulled to the sky.

POWER POSE! You may have heard about this in that famous TED Talk by Professor Amy Cuddy from Harvard. I was so over the moon when she came up with the science of the POSE – something I had been using for years. It works.

THE POWER OF THE POSE

P POSTURE

O OOMPH

S SPEECH

E EYES AND TEETH !

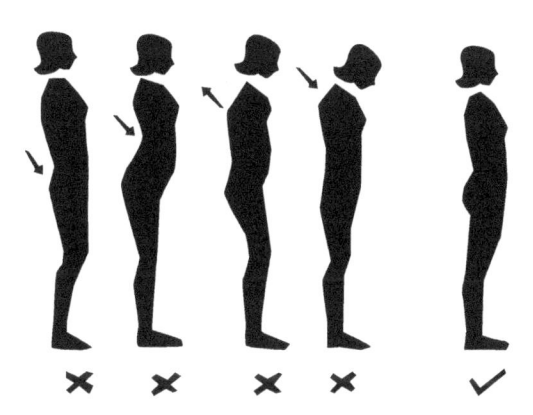

P**O**SE – O IS FOR OOMPH –

Energy, or as they say in China 加油 (jiayou), "add fuel". Do anything that gets you energised. The Visibly Brilliant ABDC activation routine in this book suggests you do something active to get your blood flowing. It works – think of 'The Haka', the war dance the New Zealand rugby team, the All Blacks, perform before their games. It's no surprise they seem to have the advantage when they fill their bodies with natural hormones including testosterone!

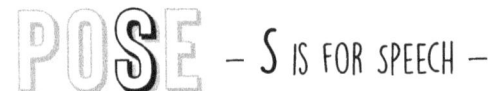

PO**S**E – S IS FOR SPEECH –

Slow down and turn the volume UP. Speech is the first thing to go if you are not feeling confident, so make sure you drink plenty of water, open your mouth and warm up your tongue if you need to. Good news... if you have a good posture, this will automatically give you a more powerful voice, and if you smile, even better, because you'll relax your jaw and give yourself more room around your vocal cords to have a fuller voice. Hey, a professionally trained voice takes years; however, my quick fix, power pose, smile and energy boost works wonders for your speech.

LOST FOR WORDS?

Quick note. If you use SIGN language instead of speech – apply all the same rules; energy, posture, smile and give it all you've got. You need very few words to make an impact! I've worked with BDA (British Deaf Association) and in my experience, sign language can be a lot more powerful and emotional than spoken words! The lesson? Use ALL your tools, make the most of what YOU have.

POSE – AND FINALLY E FOR "EYES AND TEETH!" –

In other words, SMILE. If you shout to a studio audience (like I did at the BBC) or any audience, "Eyes and teeth," you get instant, fun, energising and engaging faces beaming back at you. If YOU smile on camera, you look normal!

When you smile, your brain and your zygomatic major (cheek nerve) is turned upwards, and your brain thinks positive, happy thoughts. Opera singers smile so they maximise their vocal ability. It relaxes their vocal muscles.

So in a nutshell – the ultimate speaking hack is... eyes and teeth!

> **Twinkling TIP –** *Be YOU! If you can, stand tall, smile, let yourself shine whatever your type. If you're unable to physically stand, use whatever you have at your disposal to radiate your energy.*

★★★★★★★★★★★★★★★★★★★★★★★★★★

SAFE IN BLACK

BREAK IT UP WITH COLOUR

CHAPTER 28

WHAT TO WEAR!

★★★★★★★★★★★★★★★★★★★★★★★★★

In order to LOOK Visibly Brilliant from the outside, you need to consider your "look". Are you showing the outside world what you are really like?

Here is a quick story about the technically brilliant people who wear dark clothes and hide in the shadows not wanting to draw attention to themselves…

"I'm a navy wearer!"

… a client admitted to me recently. He had watched my TEDx talk about the hidden superheroes I call "The Invisibles" who are often found around the office wearing black or navy, so they don't stand out. They purposely wear darks, so they are NOT noticed. I used to be one of these. My entire wardrobe was SAFE-BLACK. At the BBC, I wore ASM gear without realising it. (An ASM is "Assistant Stage Manager" at the theatre or behind the scenes on any production. They always wear entirely black, so they are completely invisible when they change the set or working backstage).

Often, invisible superheroes dressed in their ASM outfits are doing more work than anyone else and by wearing black, they are deliberately not drawing attention to themselves. They'll often say things like…

"I don't need to stand out in bright colours or draw attention to myself. That's for show-offs. It's a team effort, it's not about ME, I don't need to be in the spotlight… I'm not arrogant or egotistical."

Yes, I get it. If you care about your team, lead with integrity and you are brilliant at what you do, that's fantastic. Yes, you are respected. However, why not stand out and look, sound and feel a little more "noticeable"? You're not going to lose your respect if you stand out a tiny bit more, are you?

Look, there's nothing wrong with wearing navy or black per se! However, according to experts, and my brilliant professional stylist buddy Natasha Musson, colour "pops". This is particularly important ON CAMERA/teams/Zoom/Webex. You may not CARE about the "popping"; however, if you want to look, sound and feel a little bit more... well... at the top of your game, then you need to add a splash of colour.

You DON'T need to wear:	You DO need to:
Clown-like stripes	*Be visible (if you wear only black, you disappear like the ASMs)*
BIG BOLD Blouses	
LOUD fluorescent fabrics	*Break up the DARK materials*
Flower-power shirts	*Feel confident*
The late Queen Elizabeth II's garish colours	*Feel like YOU*
Red trousers	*Dress for success – your way*
- Rupert Bear trousers	

If you speak to "colour" specialists, like the amazing Secret Stylist, Natasha Musson, (more on Natasha to follow!), you'll find very few people look good in black anyway. It doesn't always suit their natural skin tone. I had my "colours" done and I'm a cool winter jewel!

My advice to my senior leader who admitted to being a "navy wearer"? It's not just about wardrobe choices! It's about being MORE THAN just SAFE.

So, why not up your presence and impact, starting with your choice of jacket? Rather than go for the safe and slouchy same old same old… why not experiment with a shaket (that's a cross between a shirt and a jacket), or a bright accessory? How about a scarf, a statement necklace or necktie with a shade of something new?

This inspired me to write a poem!
Ode to the Navy Wearer
Break up the navy, try something new
Break up the black with a vibrant hue
Break up the grey with a golden thread
Or how about a splash of cerise, green, or red
Make dull days fresh with bold pinstripes
Colours pop, no matter what your type.

The point is, you need to be visible, so people know how brilliant you are.

What to Wear – The Professional View!

My professional style guru and good friend, the Secret Stylist Natasha Musson, shared her colour wisdom with me when I asked her about being more visible from the outside.

(The original photo was a feast of rainbow reds, yellows, pinks, and greens!)

"Why is colour so important?" I asked.

"Colour is a transmitter. Without even speaking a word, you instantly communicate to the world who you are. A splash of your favourite hue (big or small) will allow others into your personality.

"Wearing colour will instantly influence your mood and others around you. Bold bright colours will lift your spirit, and softer colours will keep your calm. We've all witnessed the fabulous person in red walking down the street on a rainy day; it sends a message of confidence and energy and brings a smile to our face.

"As a stylist who is forever in clients' homes seeking out colour to suit them, I witness their personality in the room. This can inspire you to shop for something more YOU. So, if your wardrobe is a sea of navy and black, where do you start?

"Here are my top three tips…

1. GET YOUR COLOURS DONE

Having a Colour Consultation with a professional stylist will allow you to understand the right tones and shades of colours to complement your skin tone and personality. As a stylist, I undergo a personality quiz so I can dive deep into a client's personality before I drape the colours around their face. This way, I can gage how the right colour tones and shades suit their best season. Once you've discovered whether you are warm or cool and understand your season, you can start to understand the best colour tones that suit and harmonise with you. It is like a magic wand has been placed over your face. Your eyes light up, your complexion glows – the right colours will highlight your best features.

A SPLASH OF **COLOUR** = **VISIBLY BRILLIANT**

CHECK OUT THE EBOOK FOR THE COLOUR VERSION

2. ACCESSORIES FOR BIG IMPACT

Adding a splash of colour via an accessory, such as a tie, necklace or waistcoat, is the perfect way to inject colour into your neutral wardrobe. Be brave by wearing earrings, a metallic belt or a fabulous tie. Small steps will have big impact and begin your journey of dressing more YOU.

3. TAILORING

If it fits well, you'll look better, you will feel more fabulous and like you are walking the talk! Fabulous fitting clothes tend to help you walk with confidence. Spend as much as you can on a blazer, suit or blouse to find a quality fabric and tailoring to suit YOU. Buy well, buy less and rewear it. When you know certain brands and colours that suit you, you'll find shopping easier, and you'll be able to mix/match and create more outfits.

> **"And lastly, my trendy TIP!** – *Look around your home and think about what you love in terms of colour and style. A favourite print on a mug, painting, or cushion could be your wardrobe inspiration. We often find it easier to decorate our homes with colour yet wear boring black ourselves!"*

Thank you, Natasha, for your fabulous inspiration and ideas!

★★★★★★★★★★★★★★★★★★★★★★★★★

CHUNKOLOGY

CHAPTER 29

"CHUNKOLOGY" – GATHER JUICY CHUNKS OF CONTENT EVERY DAY!

★★★★★★★★★★★★★★★★★★★★★★★★★

"Chunk It Up"

This is one of the best pieces of advice I've ever been given. And it's got nothing to do with chocolate or vomit! It's ALL about making content easy to handle so you aren't overwhelmed at the thought of creating amazing material every day. After a while, you'll find my chunkology strategy means a lot of your posts, articles, blogs and scripts are DONE FOR YOU – yay, less time, more impact, thank you very much.

No matter what you want to share, or what story you wish to tell, have ALL your content in bite-sized chunks as it's so much easier to manage, process, post and share. And the best thing? You can rinse and repeat and change up the order of the chunks to freshen it up. That's my thing, minimum effort, maximum return!

HOW DO CHUNKS WORK?

Let me give you an example of a chunk of content and how easy it is to create, using my lovely technically brilliant client from one of the "Big Four" firms, Sheera.

Sheera is about to be promoted from Senior Manager to Director and has her very nerve-wracking director panel coming up when I meet her. She's been asked to create a "business case" in order to "pitch" herself as part of the scary panel process.

Sheera has NO idea how to create, say or manage her personal elevator pitch and is all over the place when I first meet her. She tells me she's been working for a number of years at the firm in IT, very much behind the scenes, on what she calls "BIG DATA". Oooh, sounds interesting. "What's BIG DATA?" you may be wondering. In a nutshell, it is usually software on a global scale affecting multi-gazillion dollar industries.

Sheera can tell me all about the team structure and how they deliver BIG DATA software to certain deadlines. She is tremendously talented, bright and capable... yet... she has no idea how to communicate her content in a succinct, engaging and punchy manner.

I suggest we create a chunk that represents her entire business case in under 30 seconds... before she launches into the bulk of the panel interview. This is to add creditability, gravitas and personality to her "pitch", so it's not just a reading-off-slides, wooden-plank-style delivery.

What? In 30 seconds? She can't believe it's possible! Plus, this chunk is very valuable because she can use it all over the world, in meetings, dinner parties, pitches and when sitting next to a stranger on a plane.

★★★★★★★★★★★★★★★★★★★★★★★★★

This chunk strategy has changed her life… here's how we did it.

Content chunk creation using the TEEN formula…

T – Top line or the punchy headline. One of my mottos is *"Punchline at the top"*

E – Example. The story behind this is…

E – Emotion. How do you feel about this? This puts your personality into your communication and… good news… you can't be wrong!

N – Next. What's the next step? And what does it mean for the future? An easy and neat way to finish each chunk.

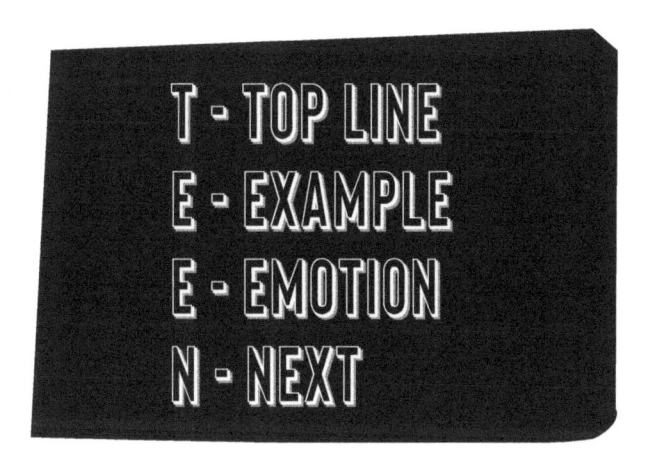

```
T - TOP LINE
E - EXAMPLE
E - EMOTION
N - NEXT
```

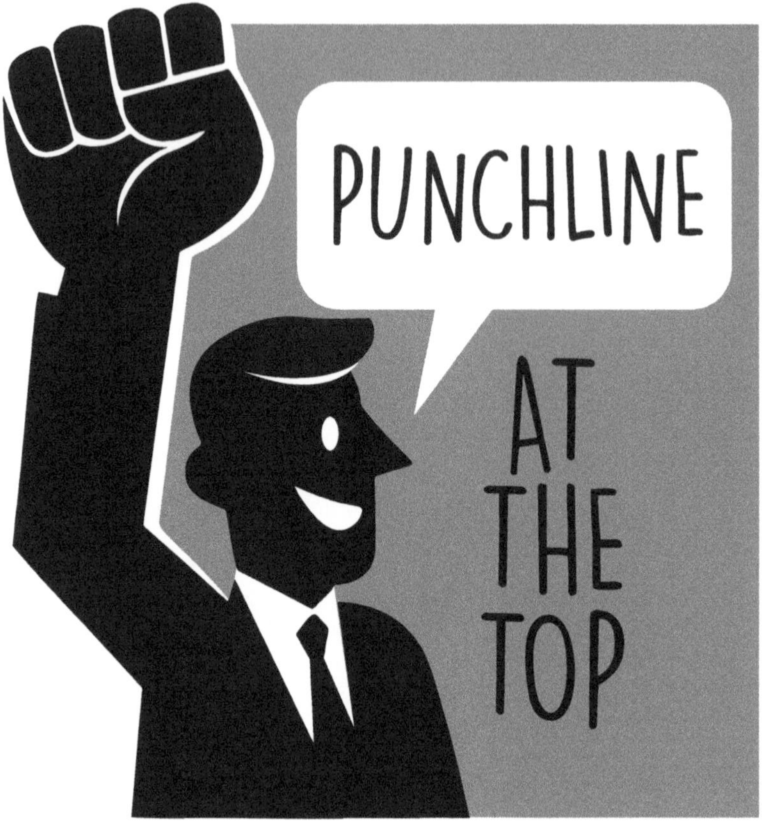
PUNCHLINE
AT THE TOP

So here's what we crafted for Sheera...

T – Top line (or the punchy headline)

"I'm excited to share with you how we're going to double our growth in the music sector with our two biggest clients using this BIG DATA software, and I predict we'll go from $4.5 million to more than $8.5 million within two years."

E – Example. The story behind this is…

Sheera mentions her close relationship with the clients over five to six years, how she's worked with them and why they are loving the new BIG DATA experience. She tells a story and a specific example.

E – Emotion. I asked Sheera, "How do you personally feel about this?…"

This puts her personality into her communication as she replies, "I feel so proud that our BIG DATA software for the music industry has been so well received."

N – Next. What's the next step? And what does it mean for the future?

An easy and neat way to finish. Sheera concludes with, "This has the potential to be a multi-billion dollar global solution, and other clients will want to jump on the bandwagon and adopt this new regime... it's exciting. The software is a gamechanger for the music business!"

> **Tailor-Made TIP – CHUNK IT UP –** *Bite-sized chunks of stuff; stories, pictures, words, paragraphs, clips, posts are much easier to digest and share. One at a time, remember, one bite at a time.*

★★★★★★★★★★★★★★★★★★★★★★★★★

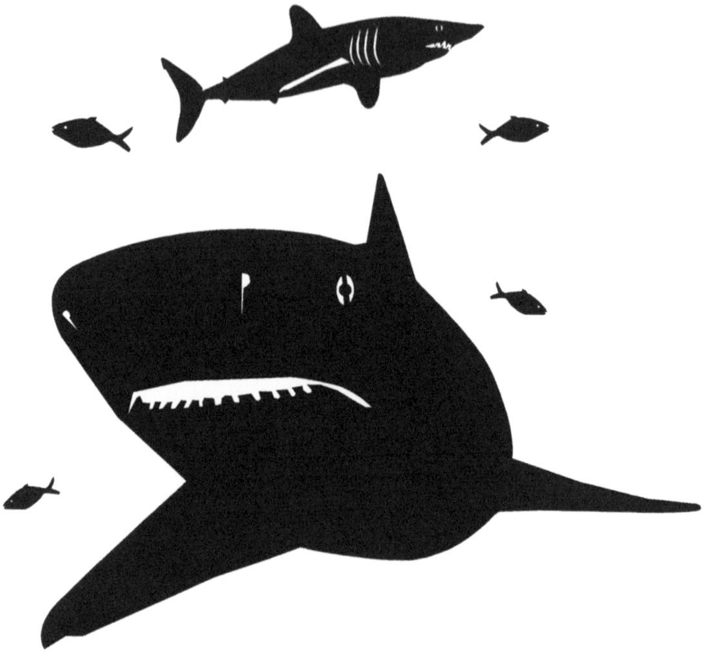

CHAPTER 30

SHARK WEEK – HOW TO CREATE YOURS!

★★★★★★★★★★★★★★★★★★★★★★★★★★★

My Story

"What's our SHARK WEEK?"

This used to be the question we'd ask ourselves in our planning meetings when, back in the days before my BBC stint, I was head of programmes at Rapture TV. We used to call any big, eye-catching set piece the "Shark Week strategy".

If you have ever watched the Discovery Channel, you will know how this works. The channel go shark-mad once a year, with a whole week full of sharks: shark films, Jaws (again!), shark documentaries, shark adverts. And they tell you about it… all year. Sharks attract big audiences; they are easy to market, and you can "hook" people in. So, Shark Week for the Discovery Channel was like clickbait.

Shark Week is the one time you get all your big guns out, show your best assets, and direct your audience to them!

At Rapture, our version of Shark Week was Ibiza club nights LIVE. We'd broadcast live from super clubs like Manumission or Pacha and advertise this from January to September as "The only LIVE clubbing night on TV!"

So, what's your personal Shark Week? That one big eye-catching project you can talk about, and which will make you shine. It's what you can bring to dinner parties, appraisals, networking events and client meetings. You need to rise above the daily grind, the noise, and the reassurance that you're great at your job. Performing well and just getting on with the job will not help you to shine or stand out. You need one big thing per year to help you raise your profile.

I was running a leadership program in a global bank recently and one of my delegates, Belle, was struggling to "get noticed".

Belle is extremely talented and brilliant at her day job. She's loyal and on the leadership track but not getting paid as much as she should. She even confided that she'd stepped up for her boss's maternity leave, held the team together, stepped in for management meetings, and did a magnificent job. She shared her ideas with the management which they loved. They used her ideas, actioned them, and she asked for nothing in return.

I suggested we adopt the Shark Week strategy!

Rather than turn resentful, it was time to act. She was doing a great job but not selling herself as an expert or a senior player. She'd made the classic mistake of expecting people around her to congratulate her on how brilliant she was and notice how much she was contributing, and therefore how much more money she deserved.

But instead, in return for her daily hard work, long hours and loyalty, she got… silence. She had no idea how to position herself and use her amazing talents to optimise her career.

We looked at how to make a Shark Week story, a big deal out of just one of her many project ideas. Her idea was all about efficiency and better communication. Trouble was, she was so busy doing it well, she had no time, energy or fuel to give it some buzz.

We decided that Belle would create a more formal presentation to share with her management team, rather than a quick round-the-table update, where her ideas were getting stolen, and her voice was not being heard.

She was terrified! Her first reaction was, *"Do you think I'll be allowed to take over a section of the ExCo meeting?"*

Well, if you don't ask, you don't get. And yes, she did ask to have a five-minute slot in the ExCo (exec committee) meeting and, yes, she did blow them away by "bigging" up one of her brilliant cost-saving, people-motivating schemes and, yes, she received a round of applause… and later on… a promotion! Hurrah!!

Quick Shark Week Exercise

Want to identify your own Shark Week? Here are three options: present, past, future.

Option 1 – Present!

What's your biggest project, promotion or event this year?

For example, for me, having a book, eBook or TEDx talk are obvious ones. However, some years my big set pieces are thin on the ground, so I pick one of my favourite client events as my Shark Week.

Option 2 – Past – If you find it hard to think of a present Shark Week – find a past one!

Think of a time when you really put yourself on the map – what did you get praised for? (or maybe you didn't get enough?)

If you had a big event, released something, or worked on a special project a year ago, maximise the impact of it. For example, if you got promoted, did a fantastic piece of work or won an award, make this your Shark Week for the next year, until you find a new shark!

Option 3 – Future – If you don't have a present or past Shark Week, create a future one.

Think of something you would LOVE to achieve, like setting up a new business, doing a collaboration with someone or partnering with a highly-respected organisation. And if you start the ball rolling on a project, this could be your future Shark Week: *"I'm working on a project with XXXX and we're looking to release it in two years."*

Jot some ideas down in your journal.

You can have a two-year Shark Week if you like – why not? Some projects span several years. In fact, my husband made a film over five years! (I must say, the Shark Week did get a bit long in the tooth!) However, life achievements don't go away.

You can always talk, write and share your insights on your cumulative Shark Weeks. Shark Weeks can last forever! Get your chops round that.

> **Shark Week TIP – CHUNK IT UP –** *Have ONE thing you can shout about each year so that you can promote it, you can look forward to it, you can talk about it, you can show off about it, ALL YEAR ROUND!*

★★★★★★★★★★★★★★★★★★★★★★★★★

PART FOUR

HOW TO KEEP UP YOUR VISIBLY BRILLIANT MOMENTUM

★★★★★★★★★★★★★★★★★★★★★★

Consistency!

Yes, you need to "do" a Visibly Brilliant activity, something every day in order to achieve Visible Brilliance long term.

I remember reading my old school reports…

"Inconsistent… she has moments of genius… but at other times she could do better…"

Aristotle caught onto this… ***"We are what we repeatedly do. Excellence then is not an act, but a habit"***

Make it a habit, and stick consistently to your one-thing-a-day... keep doing your ABCD routine in the morning.

Remember Chapter 4?

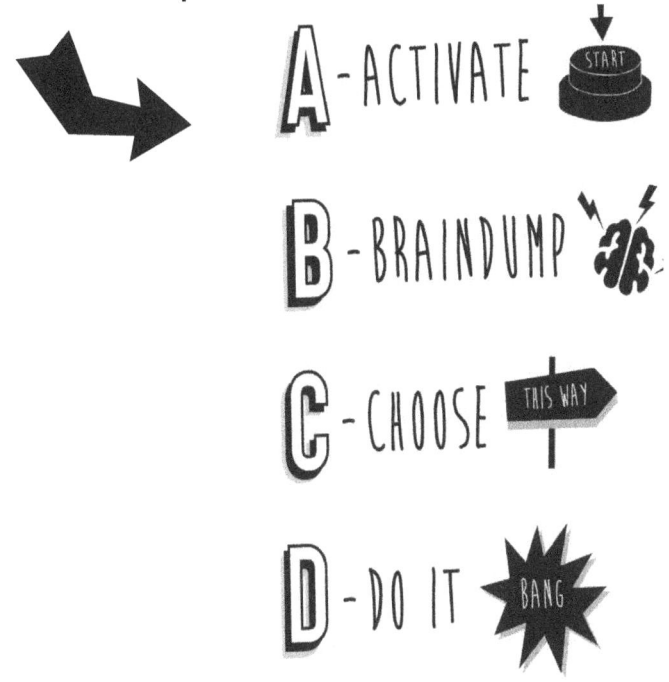

A - ACTIVATE

B - BRAINDUMP

C - CHOOSE

D - DO IT

The message here? Just do it... anything, no matter how small.

Go for it. Stand by for the Visibly Brilliant Bicycle Wheel coming up shortly.

★★★★★★★★★★★★★★★★★★★★★★★★★

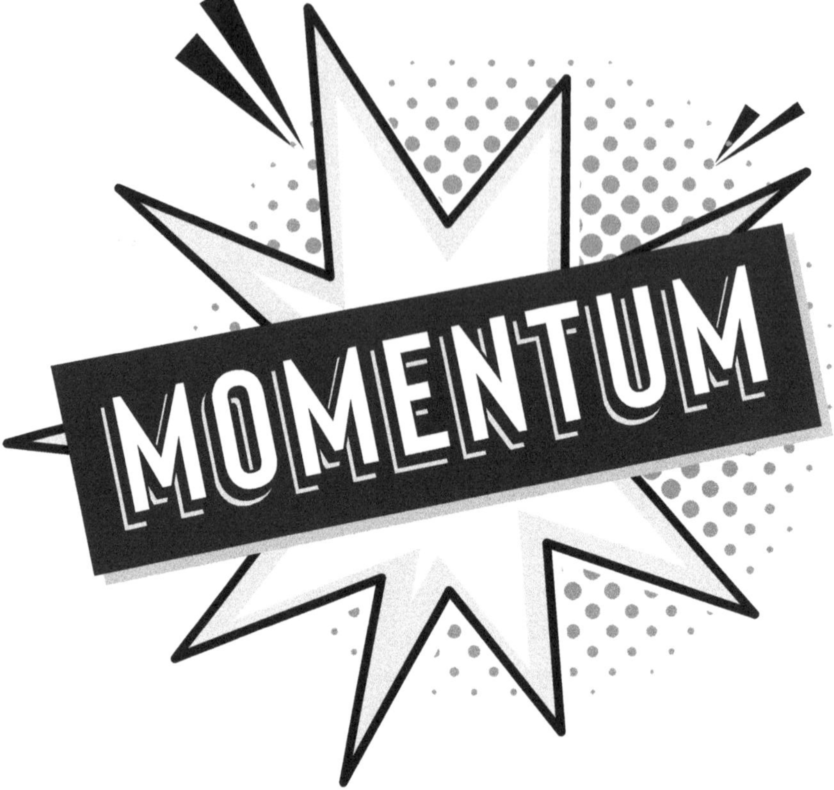
MOMENTUM

CHAPTER 31

MOMENTUM – THE VISIBLY BRILLIANT BICYCLE WHEEL

★★★★★★★★★★★★★★★★★★★★★★★★★

With all this enthusiasm about your newfound Visible Brilliance, it's essential to keep it going. No pressure here – you need to find momentum. Worried about being able to "keep it up"? Yes, that's the BIG challenge, isn't it? Consistency and momentum.

The number one thing you need in order to be Visibly Brilliant is… sustainability… i.e. long-term habits and long-terms results. And the way to achieve these is to get into regular daily routines, systems and habits that become the "norm".

My favourite daily saying is LITTLE and OFTEN. You need only do something small each day and you WILL become more visible. You'll become used to being in the spotlight, posting and even appearing in the media. However, you will need to keep the bicycle wheel of Visibility turning slowly. Then you will continue to build; like a snowball, you'll start small, and you'll get bigger and bigger, as long as you keep going.

NO PRESSURE here. The good news is you don't have to do EVERYTHING ALL AT ONCE! No, you only need to do something small!

Let me introduce you to the Visibly Brilliant Bicycle Wheel…

The list of Visibly Brilliant activities on the following pages are suggestions, NOT your to-do list! You can pick and choose which of these you'd like to get your teeth into… they are a reminder of ALL of the choices you have when it comes to being more visible.

VB BICYCLE WHEEL

- SPEAKING
- MOMENTUM

Wheel segments: PR, PICS, SOCIALS, LINKEDIN, NETWORK, NEWSLETTER, PODCAST, CONFERENCE HOST, EXTERNAL, POSTS, INTERNAL

HOST
POST
PANEL
TV
RADIO
MEDIA
ARTICLE
CHAIR
MEETING
CONFERENCE
PUBLIC SPEAKING
GUEST
NETWORKING

The good news? You only need one or two spokes to turn your wheel so don't try and do EVERYTHING NOW. Take your time. It's a slow burn.

You may be thinking, what if I:

- Run out of things to say?
- Run out of steam?
- Stall because I don't know what to post?
- Don't feel like speaking up in front of an audience?
- Can't think of anything to do today?
- Am not in the mood to be Visibly Brilliant, and just want to curl up under a stone?
- Think I'm not Visibly Brilliant and I have evidence to prove how terrible I am?

Ha, don't worry, YOU ARE HUMAN. If you feel overwhelmed, then take the day off. Yes, it's ok; step back. Sounds counter-intuitive, doesn't it? However, it's important that you enjoy your Visibly Brilliant activities and don't feel forced into the daily routine or feel guilty that you're not doing enough. You are human and I'd love to help you feel good about yourself. You're achieving so much right now, simply by reading this book!

Don't do something you really don't want to do. Please. If you don't enjoy your Visibly Brilliant activities, you WON'T do them. It's very important that you have a bit of fun with all this stuff, and you feel motivated to carry on.

If you feel a bit "meh" and unmotivated, then don't beat yourself up. Do something TINY! Maybe you could jot down a half-baked idea for an article. When you're next in the mood to write it, you'll appreciate the effort rather than the blank page. It really works! I've tried this many times myself. A half-baked idea is better than a blank page or computer screen!

Seriously, don't worry because if you have already built up a little routine to do something daily, you will already have enough lovely "stuff" bubbling away in the background and a few activities ready to complete to get your wheel to move. It doesn't matter how slowly your wheel turns. The wheel only needs one or two spokes to move – that's it!

It's ok, you are allowed to feel like crap as often as you like. I do all the time. Sometimes the last thing I feel like doing is filming a little reel or video clip for my VEA, Claire, to post. She might write an email saying,

"Hey Esther, remember to send me footage from the conference!"

And I think...

"I know, but I can't think of anything worse than having to come up with something meaningful to say right now. I'm tired. I'm a little bit stressed about the conference. Oh shit, I need to pick up food for the kids on the way home and my brain won't let me feel free and creative right now... help!"

Many business leaders and entrepreneurs feel the same, because guess what? We are human. Yes, we are not perfect, creative, and up for it all of the time.

SO, account for your OFF days. It's ok, that's why you have set yourself in motion. Your wheel and your daily activities allow you to take a day off or a week off and DO NOTHING because you've already put into place your Visibly Brilliant structure.

Once you have momentum, you're off. Go slow.

My Story

I was sharing my fear of "lack of momentum" with Jacq Burns, my writing guru and agent, on one of her legendary writing retreats. I confessed that MOMENTUM was the one thing I found a struggle with when writing this book.

I confessed:

"When I stop writing everyday – or break the cycle of focusing on Visibly Brilliant for a short period of time – I stall, I go blank, I procrastinate. For some reason my wheel stops turning, I lose faith in my ideas, I doubt myself and forget what I've written. I find it hard to keep up the momentum."

I looked at Jacq Burns in the eyes hoping for the answer to my big question.

"What's wrong with me?"

Ha, I knew the answer already. Nothing is wrong. It's life getting in the way!! Hence, we have our routines, processes, and quite frankly, mundane scheduling activities in place.

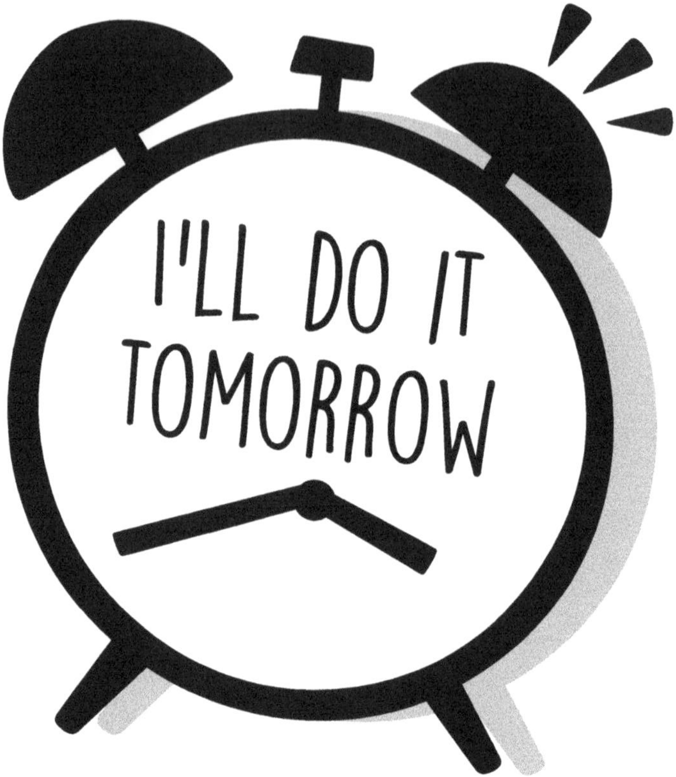
I'LL DO IT
TOMORROW

This ABCD routine IS so important because it keeps the wheel oiled. (To remind you it stands for: Activate, Brain Dump, Choose, Do It.) Even if you don't see immediate results, you will. Long term, you will reap the rewards.

Jacq confessed that she finds keeping up her Visibly Brilliant momentum a challenge as she has been taking my advice and working towards being Visibly Brilliant since working on this book with me. The following conversation made me laugh. She was complaining about the recent photoshoot she had done – because I always say to people who want to raise their profile and be Visibly Brilliant…

"*You can never have too many good photos of yourself!*"

Jacq said she didn't look her best the day she had her photos done. She'd invested in these amazing pictures by a professional photographer.

My reaction?

"There's no such thing as ONE photoshoot… take photos as often as you can!"

All you need is to sprinkle a little bit of your brilliance into the public domain or your intranet at work to remind people you exist.

All you need is a tiny bit of wheel action, and the spokes will turn.

> **Teeth and eyes TIP –** *If you have a high-profile speech, presentation, town hall meeting, article, awards do, always make sure you get several photos or images. And guess what? You can use this ONE BIG enthusiastic flurry!*

★★★★★★★★★★★★★★★★★★★★★★★★★

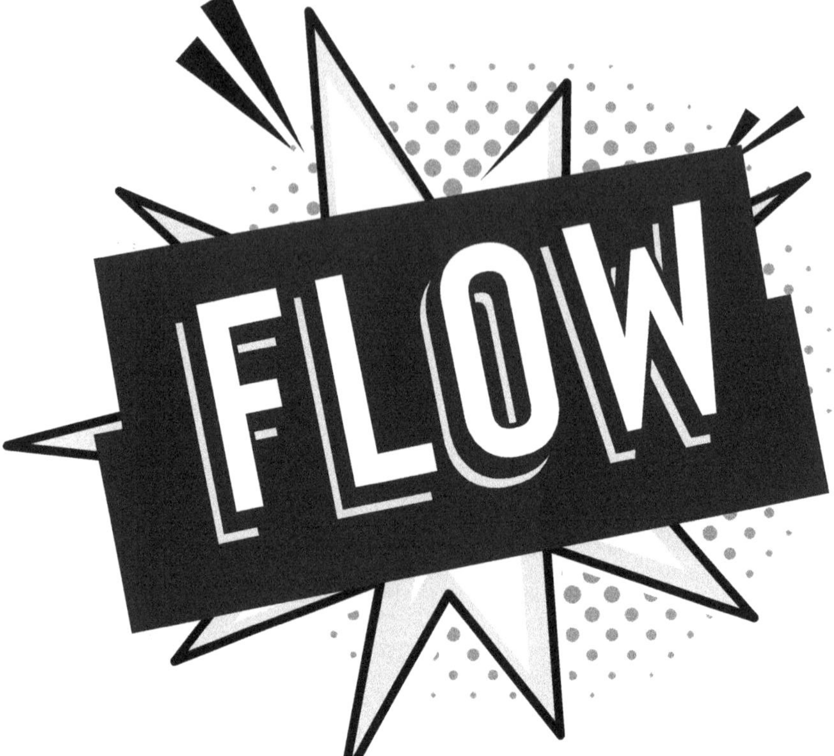
FLOW

CHAPTER 32

FLOW - FEEL YOUR VISIBLY BRILLIANT MOTION!

★★★★★★★★★★★★★★★★★★★★★★★★★

Flow is what we're looking for. You'll know when you're *"in flow,"* a term used by psychologists to describe that peak performance when you are immersed in your practice, and everything clicks into place for you. You can feel it when you are moving at the perfect pace; posting, presenting or "podding" (appearing on a podcast!). You are in motion.

You'll also feel it when you start to move too fast and your Visibly Brilliant bicycle wheel starts to spin. It's a good idea not to get dizzy! You don't want to burn out, you want to remain in control. Slow and steady, little and often, will always get you to your destination in a sustainable and chilled out fashion!

My good friend John Spencer Williams, author of "F*ck Work, Let's Play" works with entrepreneurs all the time and helps them market themselves on LinkedIn.

Many of his entrepreneurs tell him, *"I get no traction on LinkedIn."*

He tells them, *"Post regularly, and you will get a response."*

The trouble is, John tells me, when people are launching their new idea, new role, or new business, they have a splurge of activity, a flurry of enthusiasm. They post loads of stuff, they have a whoosh of energy and focus; pictures, articles, posts and they tag in lots of people.

"Woo-hoo, look at me, I'm doing this great new shiny thing!"

★★★★★★★★★★★★★★★★★★★★★★★★★★★

Teeny Steps TIP – *Visibly Brilliant people need the "little and often" approach for the long term. It doesn't matter how slowly you go. You just need to GO. If you have a flurry or shove a hundred things out there in one go, you WILL be visible for a day, but then your visibility will fall off a cliff.*

★★★★★★★★★★★★★★★★★★★★★★★★★★★

John says it's fine and dandy that week, when they post loads of material. Yet, when they stop posting after the splurge, things drop off, the activity goes quiet, then they complain they're not getting any traction. According to John, the **"algorithms don't like that feast or famine"** approach. People are too impatient.

Look, don't let this put you off LinkedIn; I too find LinkedIn and Instagram hateful at times because of that feeling of emptiness when the tumbleweed hits after a "like, like" peak.

It's purely an illustration of how you need to keep the wheel turning slowly but surely. Little and often. Be patient. Keep going, never give in!

Your Visibly Brilliant wheel needs to be oiled and added to. No one said you must have topical, beautiful, perfectly formed NEW material every single day. You won't be firing on all cylinders every single day, and that's ok. You are human.

However, when you are firing on all cylinders, create a few posts, articles, photos, ideas for future newsletters, presentations, posts, or keynote speeches.

Here are some of the many things (post and talking point ideas) you can add to your Visibly Brilliant wheel...

- Coming up next month
- "Throwback Thursday" anyone?
- At the bottom of your email – "Proud winner of..."
- In two, three, four years, "on this day..."
- RINSE AND REPEAT, REPURPOSE, REUSE stuff you already have! (You'll soon store it up!)

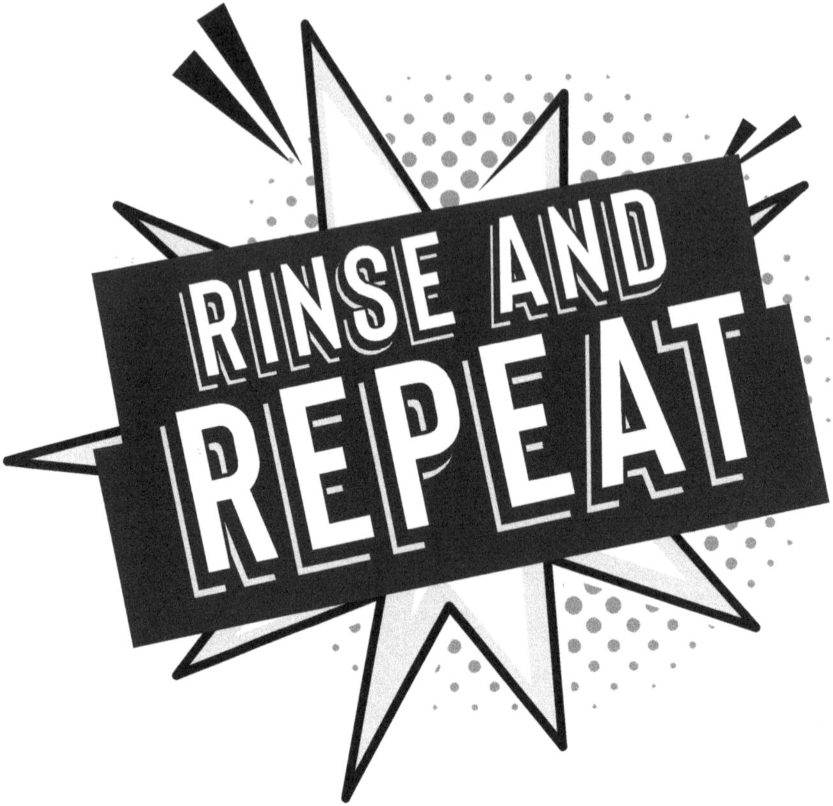
RINSE AND
REPEAT

CHAPTER 33

SUCCESS! WHAT DOES IT LOOK LIKE?

★★★★★★★★★★★★★★★★★★★★★★★★★

What is Visibly Brilliant success anyway?

There's no "end point" or "I've made it!" moment. I'm never "finished", a bit like my to-do list. I'm always working on my next project and keeping the wheels of visibility oiled.

I used to picture myself relaxing on a yacht, Martini in hand and that was my definition of "made it". Even when I have been at the Cannes Film Festival or at a glitzy award ceremony, I've never felt, "The job is done... I now pronounce myself ...successful."

I am probably partially Visibly Brilliant but not 100%... The job is never done; however, if you want to grow, boost or run a business or climb the career ladder... you do need to find a daily habit to help you to be visible or you might end up stuck.

Imagine taking a holiday on that yacht drinking your Martini without that low level panic at the back of your mind...

"What if they take the credit while I'm away", or "What if I miss out on a new client because I'm not there to jump when they say jump?"

I'm writing this book, not because I've made it, but because I, like you, am one of "The Invisibles" who's coming out... slowly, not always getting it right... and when I do progress, it makes me want to share my knowledge and encourage others to join me!

A Success Story – Su Bei

Su Bei was brilliant in so many ways. She worked long hours and had studied hard to get her internship at a leading media agency. On paper, she had more academic qualifications than all her colleagues put together. She was a typical OD-er (over-deliverer), and a dream to work with. She'd be at her desk before everyone else, she was loyal, you could trust her with budgets, forward planning and if someone was off sick, she would always fill in.

Su Bei was technically brilliant at her job. However, when it came to being Visibly Brilliant – i.e. speaking up and getting noticed – she was too busy grinding away at her work to be seen and fully recognised for her talents.

And then one day Su Bei had a shocking wake-up call.

A much younger, less-experienced colleague, Marc, was promoted above her and became her boss.

Su Bei was completely deflated. She'd worked so hard and assumed that she'd get the senior role she "deserved" because she was a loved, loyal and diligent worker. But she didn't... and when she expressed her distress to a colleague, she had a major a-ha moment; she realised she'd been brilliant, but invisible. She was indeed one of the secret superheroes – one of "The Invisibles" – so she decided there and then to do something about it.

Rather than become angry and resentful towards Marc, she decided to up her game and change the way people perceived her. Together we cooked up a plan to create an event that she could host and make her own. That way she could be seen, heard and recognised for her talents!

She was already on the diversity committee but had never put herself forward to speak or host anything. She'd usually opted for helping with the name badges or serve welcoming drinks!

At first, she was afraid to be the person at the front of the room welcoming the guest speakers. Wow, how things have changed. She now hosts her popular networking breakfast once a month, AND she hosts panels and speaks herself – something she NEVER would have done before. Now she owns her space and she's walking the talk as the go-to diversity spokesperson for her organisation. She's Visibly Brilliant.

Su Bei learnt to feel good about raising her profile, got herself out there, then was promoted, effortlessly stepping into a leadership role and became the go-to spokesperson. And lived happily ever after! (You get the picture!)

Su Bei's story is a common one. I meet talented, hardworking people like her all the time who get stuck behind their desk, working overtime and missing out on professional opportunities to move their career and business forward.

> **Tuned in TIP** – *Take the bull by the horns and create an easy-to-organise gig. A breakfast, lunch and learn, or maybe interview a leader in your field and create a vlog?*

★★★★★★★★★★★★★★★★★★★★★★★★★

204

CHAPTER 34

MY FINAL STORY

★★★★★★★★★★★★★★★★★★★★★★★★

Have you read Su Bei's story? Remember, that used to be me! I had what looked like the most glamorous job in the world, in showbiz, interviewing celebs. Yet, on the inside I was scared to be Visibly Brilliant and stayed firmly within my comfort zone. At the BBC I'd produce daily live shows, come up with ideas, write scripts and brief talent. I loved it. It was easy to justify my busy schedule as I put all my energy into my daily job. However, I was afraid to show off my own talent outside my role. Looking back, I think it was because of my fear of being found out as not good enough.

The funny thing is, I knew what to do. After 20 years of helping others to shine live on air at the BBC, on radio and TV, I had every trick in the book to look, sound and feel confident but it hadn't occurred to me to apply these tricks and techniques to myself.

I had another wake-up call when I set up my own business as The Impact Guru to help my clients to be Visibly Brilliant. I was asked to speak at a legal event in London in front of 200 lawyers and I had a massive shock. I realised I'd hit another moment of Visibly Brilliant anxiety, and again I had to face up to the fact I had avoided the spotlight my whole life. I hadn't realised how terrified I was of public speaking. It was a crippling moment for me as I knew this was something I had to master to run my business.

I knew I had to change if I was to make my business work. I knew I had to become an accomplished speaker. I had to become Visibly Brilliant.

It was time to face my fear, take my own advice and STEP INTO THE SPOTLIGHT myself. It was a scary time. I had to dig deep, face my insecurities, "fess-up" to my inner demons and accept I had to deal with some baggage to move on and walk my talk! So I did, and I survived the ordeal.

Many of my very senior clients feel this discomfort too and that's why I'm driven to help them. They tell me that the thought of "getting themselves out there" makes them want to run for the hills! I hope that what you have discovered through reading my book is that you can be Visibly Brilliant without a personality transplant, that you can gain confidence by pushing through your fears and venturing outside your comfort zone, even if you are the sort of person who hates the spotlight. I used to hate having all eyes on me. I used to be afraid of public speaking, but I practiced and got better and better and less afraid. Now I do it for a living. Can you believe it? Speaking in public IS my comfort zone.

I am ok with being Visibly Brilliant now. I am ok with sharing. I'm happy to share my life lessons, tips, secrets and experience with you!

SO… before you go and conquer the world now you are a Visibly Brilliant superhero… one last story…

The other day I had to chuckle to myself. My co-host at a conference in London, Sara (a fantastic live presenter), who's a respected senior editor at a publishing house, confessed,

"Esther, I've been covering this up. I'm not as confident as you, I don't think I'll ever be as confident as you on stage, you make it seem so effortless!"

Ha, ha, ha , OMG where do I start?! I replied,

"I may look effortless. The only way I can make this seem easy is because I feel the fear and do it anyway. I am not effortlessly confident, I still struggle with my inner confidence, self-belief and fear of being found out… sometimes I just smile and wave. I've put a lot of effort into being effortless. Sometimes I am winging it, I'm making this up as I go along, I'm pretending to be confident. Maybe it's me who's covering it up, not you, Sara. You are bloody awesome!"

No one gets it right all of the time. Most of the leaders I have the pleasure of working with don't think they are good enough, are afraid that somehow they are a fraud and don't feel effortlessly confident, even when they are calling the shots for thousands of people all over the world.

> **Toodles TIP** – *Sometimes all you need to do is show up and smile.*

Cue YOU. That's it. You are ready to go. Fly, my friend, take off. Spread your Visibly Brilliant wings and soar into the sky. Don't worry if you're still feeling a little shaky and in need of keeping your stabilisers on... that's normal. You're almost there!

You may be feeling:

Worried and guilty that you've taken so long to be Visibly Brilliant. You've dragged your feet, and now you're annoyed at yourself for having what feels like a mountain to climb.

My tip? Stop beating yourself up! You are doing fine. SO what? You are starting now. Well done, better late than never! Don't give up. Come on, let's get to base camp!

Questioning yourself, saying "Can I (little old me) be Visibly Brilliant?" Like Eve who the other day said to me, "Can you believe little old me from a council estate in East London, who never went to uni, was telling the CEO, COO and CFO what to do with the staff structure?!"

My reaction? "Yes, Eve, you are Head of HR! You are not little, you are massively experienced, you have a powerful voice. Who cares where you are from?"

Powerful – that's good! You now have the Visibly Brilliant toolkit, including the Triple A Formula and the Visibly Brilliant bicycle wheel of momentum and the daily routine to use, and that is empowering. You know what you are good at, how to put your brilliant content chunks together to share with the outside world and you are feeling better than the invisible grinder you once were. You have given yourself permission to accept yourself and what you offer your business and that's a great feeling.

Ready to roll! Yay, Carpe Diem – seize the day, life's too short not to get yourself out there and take on the world. You are **READY NOW** to share your brilliance, speak in public, post articles, strut your stuff, sashay into the meeting and wear that well-tailored blazer that makes you look a million bucks. You have embodied the Visibly Brilliant daily routine and everything it stands for. You have **ARRIVED**. Fabulous, darling. I love that you have come this far!

What's next? Hurrah, you have officially **ARRIVED** and now you want to thrive. Yes, you shall. Where do you go from here? What can you do to continue this feeling of euphoria, confidence, and motivation to step into the spotlight?

> **Touching TIP** – *I know it's hard to believe in yourself. However, believe me, dear reader – you are not "little old me", you are an experienced and brilliant expert who has worked hard your entire career. You've also taken the time to read this book because you know you are better than the invisible worker who's solely focused on the daily grind!*

BELIEVE THIS:

You are bloody brilliant.
Why shouldn't you share yourself with the world?

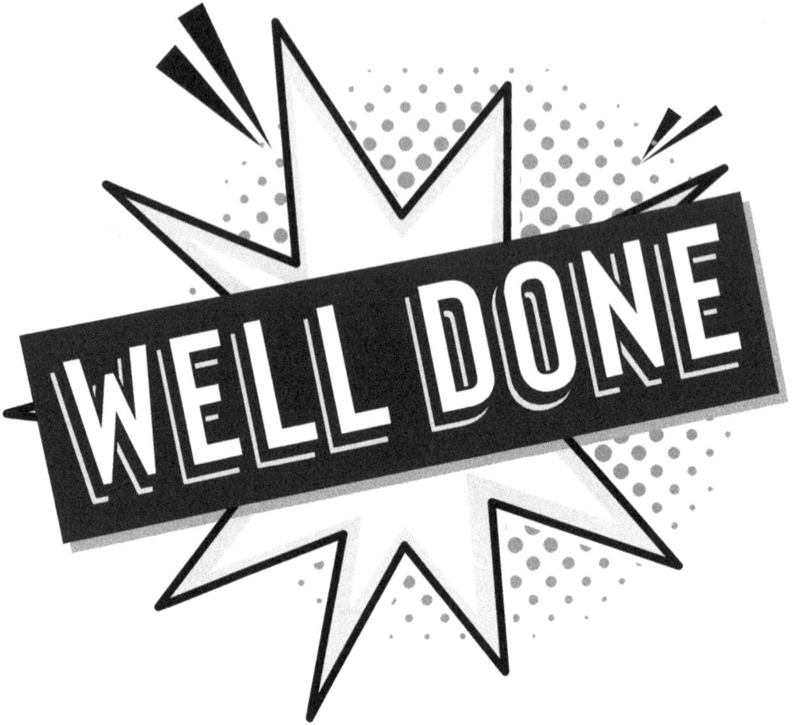
WELL DONE

★★★★★★★★★★★★★★★★★★★★★★★★

WELL DONE for reading this book and coming on this adventure with me. There's NOTHING holding you back now. Come on, break open the bubbly and let's celebrate!

You are READY to show the world (and your boss) how talented you are!

Eyes and teeth.

Love Esther x

★★★★★★★★★★★★★★★★★★★★★★★★

Tickle Me Pink TIP – *Come and join others from all over the world on the online program. It will keep you on track. Here are the details.*

The Visibly Brilliant program can be found at
www.visiblybrilliant.com
www.estherstanhope.com

References/Further Reading over a cuppa!

People – OMG, I couldn't do this without you:
Business Coach: Kim Duke

Olivia James – Performance & Confidence Coach
Juliet Blanch – amazing lawyer

Mutta – professional in London – you have the biggest heart

TEDx Talk by **Professor Amy Cuddy** from Harvard

Natasha Musson – The Secret Stylist website: *www.natashamusson.co.uk*

★★★★★★★★★★★★★★★★★★★★★★★★★

Books I mentioned – you'll love them too!

Gill Whitty-Collins, **Why Men Win at Work**, Luath Press, 2021

Zena Everett, **The Crazy Busy Cure**, John Murray Business, 2022,

Zena Everett, **Mind Flip: Take the fear out of your career**, Curlew House, 2020

Stephen R Covey, **The 7 Habits of Highly Effective People**, Simon & Schuster, 2020

John Spencer Williams, **F*ck Work, Let's Play**, Pearson Business, 2020

Aesop's Fables, **The Hare and the Tortoise**, Penguin Classics, 1998

ACKNOWLEDGEMENTS – Cheers, big ears!

★★★★★★★★★★★★★★★★★★★★★★★★★

YOU – THANK YOU for reading this book and thank you for following my stuff!

Patrick Volavka – for the amazing design and graphics – TOP DRAW!

Jacq Burns, the brilliant founder of the London Writers Club and my personal writing coach

Claire Holmes – for being there to pick up the pieces EVERYDAY

Olivia Eisinger – the most amazing editor – you have your head screwed on

Zara Thatcher – super cool, super calm, super collected

Margo Wardorf – inspirational

Maria Aldous – supportive all the way

Rowan Ahmadi-Nameghi – my guiding star

Kirsty and Kristina from Simplero

Jem, Elia and Claudio – For helping with my TEDx – priceless advice

★★★★★★★★★★★★★★★★★★★★★★★★★

My family: Adam, Mirabelle and Truman, plus the entire Dixon clan for being there from the beginning.

THANK YOU

LET'S CONNECT

If you want more tips, blogs and my fun video tips,
do go to my website.

You'll love it.

Website: **www.estherstanhope.com**

LinkedIn: **Please connect with me**

Email: **impact@estherstanhope.com**

NOTES

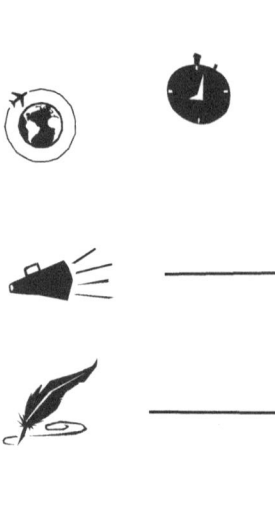

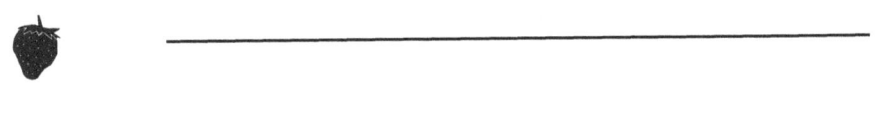

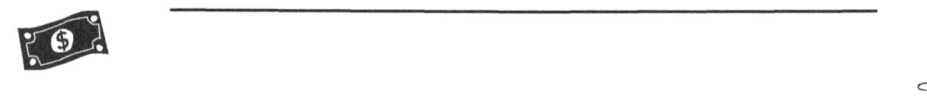

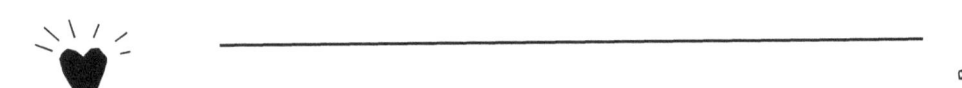

NOTES

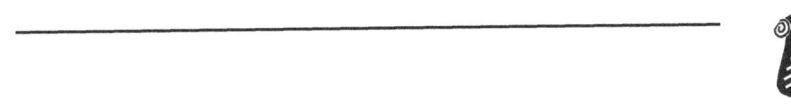

NOTES

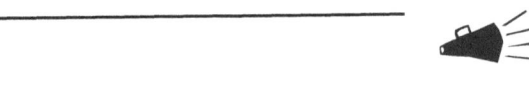

NOTES

NOTES

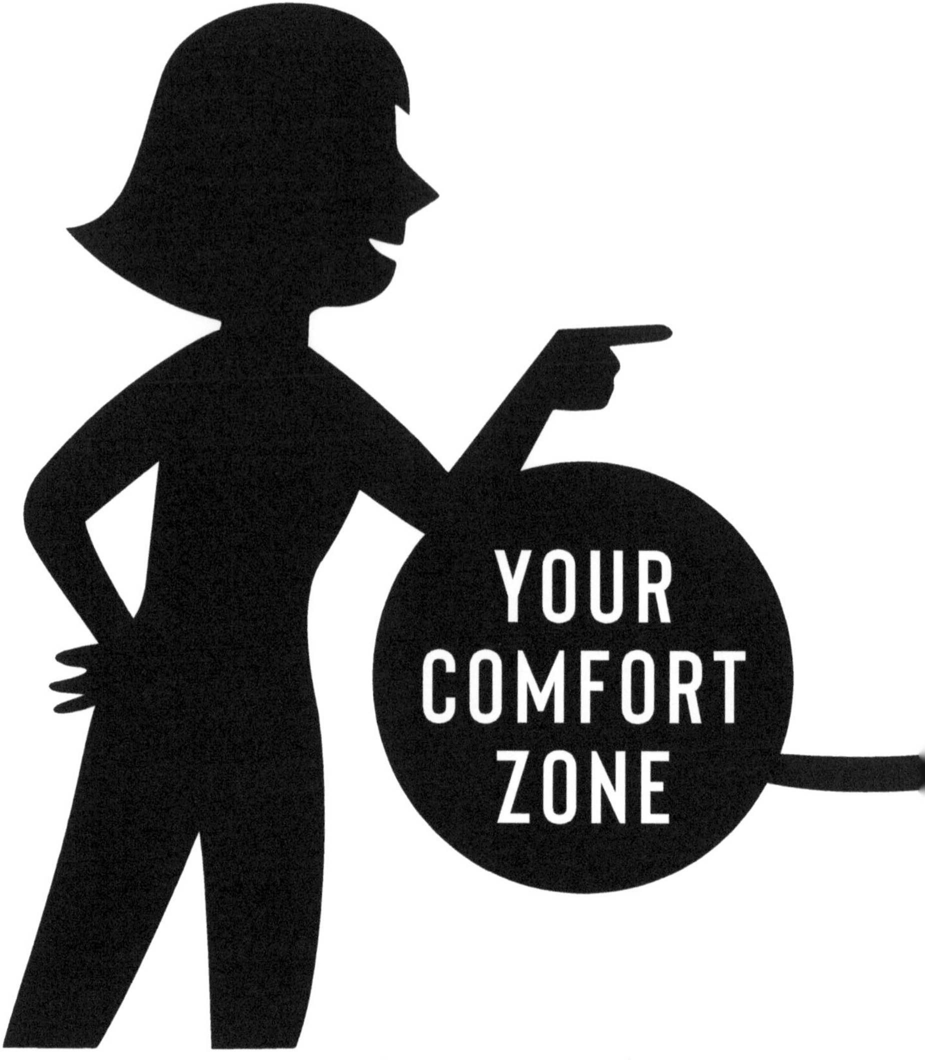
YOUR
COMFORT
ZONE

WHERE THE MAGIC HAPPENS

The Final TIP – *sometimes all you need to do is show up and smile.*
#Eyes and teeth!

ABOUT THE AUTHOR

Award-winning author, TEDx speaker, personal impact expert, and former "Invisible".

Esther Stanhope was named The Impact Guru by her client, Deloitte, because of her ability to give people instant impact when they speak. She helps business leaders, politicians, techies, lawyers and creative talent from all over the world to have more "personal impact". With a background in live broadcasting (10 years at the BBC) and nurturing on-air talent, her USP is… she can get a good performance out of anyone!

Esther gives people the confidence to be themselves and nurture their innate talent to increase their visibility. She helps them venture far outside their comfort zone and achieve what feels like the impossible.

Her first book "Goodbye Glossophobia: Banish your fear of public speaking" won Highly Commended at the Business Book of the Year Award 2020. It sold out on Amazon on day three!

Based in Spitalfields, London, Esther is a mum of two, is married to feature-film producer Adam Stanhope, has a cat, and plays the alto saxophone.

Her claim to fame? She's interviewed hundreds of celebs and stars including Madonna and George Clooney, plus she's worked alongside three Prime Ministers LIVE on air.

She's one of six children and lost her father aged five, so found herself quietly running the family home at a very young age in West London. For many years, she was invisibly brilliant, but never felt she was anything special. She didn't have the confidence to venture outside her comfort zone and into the spotlight, until she left the BBC and started her own business in her 40s. That's why she's driven to help "The Invisibles" (the quietly brilliant people behind the scenes) to get out there and share themselves with the world.

Get in touch with Esther:
esther@estherstanhope.com